People weekly

YEARBOOK

THE YEAR IN REVIEW: 1996

Copyright 1997 Time Inc. Home Entertainment

Published by

A division of Time Inc. Home Entertainment
1271 Avenue of the Americas
New York NY 10020

PEOPLE WEEKLY is a registered trademark of Time Inc.
ISBN: 1-883013-10-0
Manufactured in the United States of America

PEOPLE YEARBOOK 1997
EDITOR: Eric Levin
SENIOR EDITOR: Richard Burgheim
ART DIRECTOR: Anthony Kosner
WRITERS: Elizabeth Cohen, Thomas Fields-Meyer,
Andrew Sprung
PICTURE EDITOR: Josef Siegle
CHIEF OF RESEARCH: Denise Lynch
COPY EDITOR: Ricki Tarlow
OPERATIONS: Michelle Lockhart

Special thanks to Alan Anuskiewicz, Michael G. Aponte, Robert Britton, John Calvano, Steven Cook, Brien Foy, David Geithner, Suzanne Golden, Erikka Haa, Penny M. Hays, George Hill, Patricia R. Kornberg, Eric Mischel, James Oberman, Stephen Pabarue, Matthew Semble, Celine Wojtala and the Edit Tech staff.

PEOPLE CONSUMER MARKETING
VICE PRESIDENT: Jeremy Koch
CIRCULATION DIRECTOR: Greg Harris
ASST. CONSUMER MARKETING DIRECTOR: Bill Barber
MARKETING MANAGER: Maureen O'Brien

TIME INC. NEW BUSINESS DEVELOPMENT
DIRECTOR: David Gitow
ASSOCIATE DIRECTOR: Stuart Hotchkiss
FULFILLMENT MANAGER: Michelle Gudema
DEVELOPMENT MANAGERS: Robert Fox, Michael Holahan.
Jennifer McLyman, John Sandklev, Alicia Wilcox
EDITORIAL OPERATIONS MANAGER: John Calvano
PRODUCTION MANAGER: Donna Miano-Ferrara
ASSISTANT PRODUCTIN MANAGER: Jessica McGrath
PRODUCTION CONSULTANT: Joseph Napolitano
FINANCIAL MANAGER: Tricia Griffin
ASSISTANT FINANCIAL MANAGER: Heather Lynds
ASSOCIATE DEVELOPMENT MANAGERS: Ken Katzman, Daniel
Melore, Allison Weiss, Dawn Weland
ASSISTANT DEVELOPMENT MANAGERS:
Alyse Daberko, Charlotte Siddiqui
Marketing Assistant: Lyndsay Jenks

Title Page: Margaux Hemingway, 1982

FACE TIME

A LAUGH (SHE'S THE ONE!), A GRIN (WE GOT THE GOLD, BABY!), A STOIC MASK (YES, I LIED). MANY OF THE YEAR'S MOST COMPELLING STORIES WERE CAPTURED IN THE BEACON OF A FACE, FROM THE AGONY OF THE MOTHERS OF DUNBLANE TO THE BOOGIE OF A RUSSIAN BEAR

At Long Last Love

The ecstatic state of their union was suggested in June when the world's most eligible bachelor, 35, and his leading lady, 30, were photographed at a benefit for the Robin Hood Foundation at the New York Hilton. Elegant and free-spirited, the 6'-tall Carolyn Bessette from White Plains, New York, had reportedly met JFK Jr. in 1992 while jogging in Central Park, during his Daryl Hannah days. This year, the couple exhibited some very public peaks and valleys—arguing in Central Park in February (he pulled a ring off her hand), later kissing and partying all over Manhattan. Despite intense scrutiny, the former Calvin Klein publicist and her man managed to surprise the world when they wed on a remote island in Georgia in September (see Family Matters). Turns out the two had been engaged for more than a year.

Executive Privilege

In the novels of Jane Austen, savvy young heroines overcome barriers of class and money to win the men of their dreams; in real life, people usually settle for what is available. In the case of Gwyneth Paltrow, 23, what is available seems like a dream. In August, the lovely daughter of actress Blythe Danner and TV producer-director Bruce Paltrow took her leading man, actor and superhunk Brad Pitt, 32, and her movie, *Emma* (adapted from the Austen novel), all the way to 1600 Pennsylvania Avenue, where it was screened by President Clinton. He apologized for his wife and daughter (who were off scouting colleges), saying they wished they were there because "they love Jane Austen." Paltrow was wowed. "I've been to Washington," she said, "but never like this."

CONTENTS

Kerri Strug mends (see page 31)

**Brad Pitt and
Gwyneth Paltrow
step out
(see page 6)**

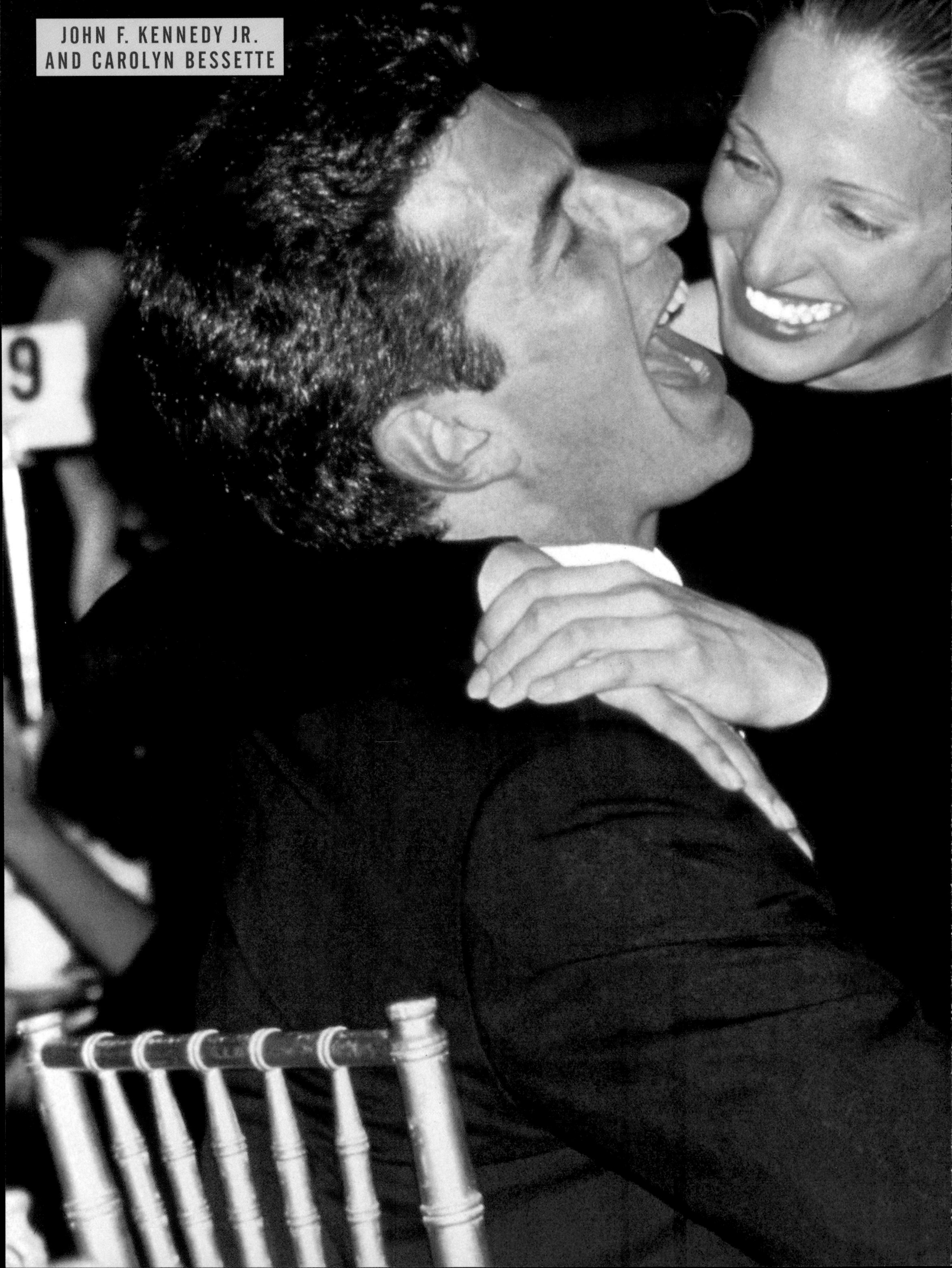

JOHN F. KENNEDY JR.
AND CAROLYN BESSETTE

Global Warming

The Golden Globe Awards, in January, have become more than a tune-up (and often a bellwether) for the Oscars, which follow in March. Bestowing favor on the glitterati of TV as well as film, the Globes are now Hollywood's first mega-event of the year, a major magnet for stars, who are often just as intrigued with each other as the public and press are with them. At a post-ceremony bash at Paramount, Kidman—named best actress in a comedy for *To Die For*—chatted with Foster, while Kidman's hubby, Tom Cruise, enjoyed zero degrees of separation from an unknotted Kevin Bacon.

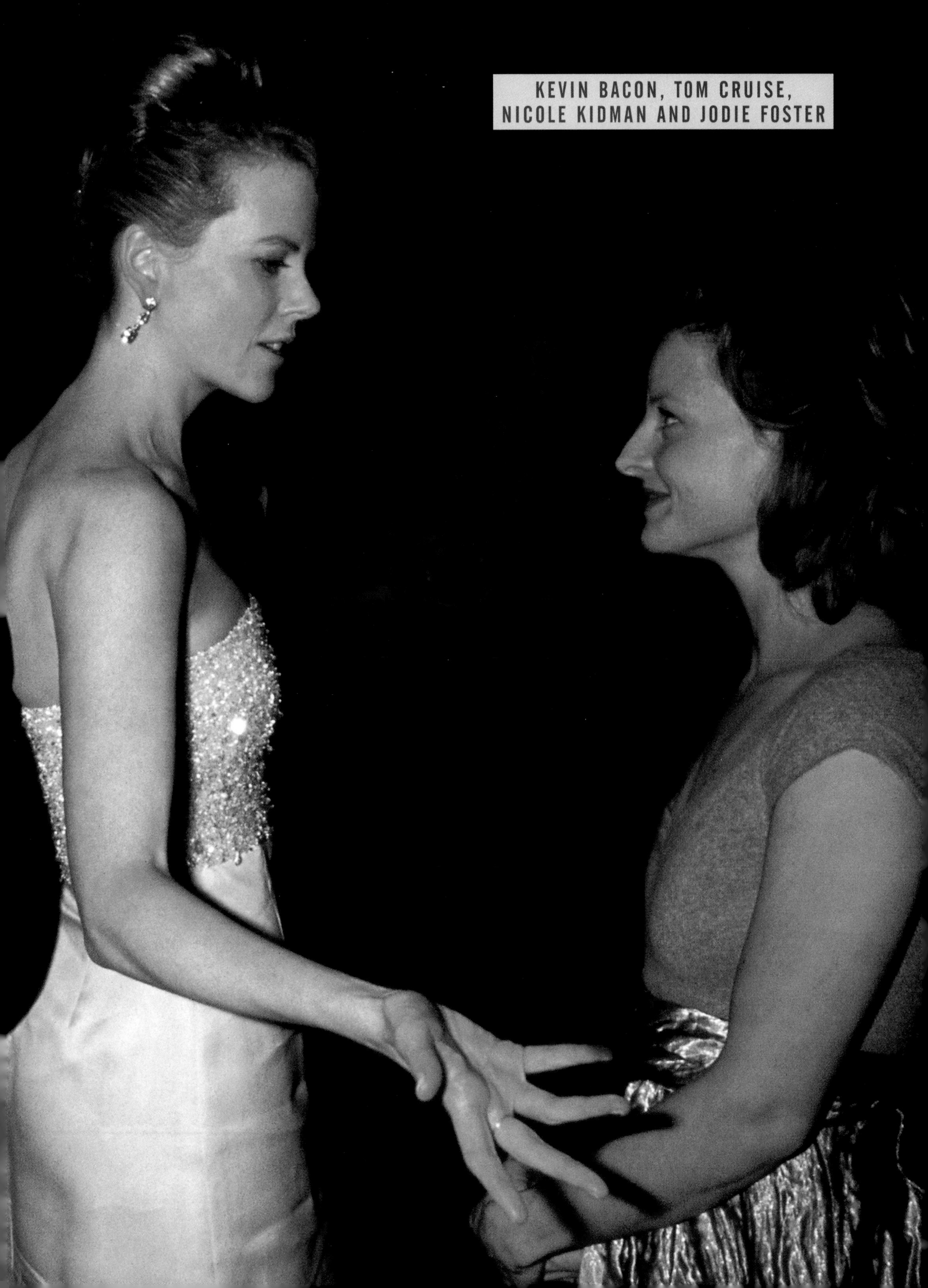

KEVIN BACON, TOM CRUISE,
NICOLE KIDMAN AND JODIE FOSTER

Hear Them Roar

American women performed brilliantly at the Atlanta Games, claiming golds in soccer, softball, basketball and track events including the 4x100 and 4x400 relays. The 4x100 team (shown here) included Miller, whose sprinter dad Lennox was also an Olympic medalist, and hometown hero Torrence, who was raised in an Atlanta housing project.

INGER MILLER, GAIL DEVERS,
CHRYSTE GAINES AND GWEN TORRENCE

Shock Waves

Centennial Olympic Park had become the social center of the Atlanta Games—a place to mingle and celebrate, accessible to all—when at 1:25 a.m. on July 27, 10 days after the crash of TWA Flight 800, a pipe bomb hidden in a knapsack detonated, sending shrapnel flying through a crowd of dancers at the park and shattering again America's tattered sense of safety. NBC cameras captured the chaotic aftermath, as volunteers rushed to aid the 110 injured and reporters swarmed the scene. The blast claimed the life of 44-year-old Alice Hawthorne, an entrepreneur and cable-TV service rep from Albany, Georgia, who had brought her daughter, Fallon Stubbs, to the park as a treat on her 14th birthday. Fallon was injured but recovered. The toll would have been higher had not a security guard reported the suspicious knapsack and helped clear the area, beginning his own Olympic nightmare (see Headliners).

OLYMPIC BOMBING

School Bussing

When is a kiss just a kiss? Not in U.S. elementary schools. When Johnathan Prevette, 6 (left), pecked a fellow first-grader on the cheek, he was promptly suspended from his Lexington, North Carolina, class. In a world where "political correctness" often seems to have run amok, the punishment of Johnathan and also of a kissing 7-year-old from New York City, and the labeling of their acts as "sexual harassment," were widely ridiculed. But for the kissees—those on the opposite end of the uninvited lips—the experience can be traumatizing. For California sixth-grader Tianna Ugarte, schoolyard taunts and threats became so frightening that her family sued the unresponsive school and won $500,000. This thorny new issue of school bussing—and liability—now seems headed for the Supreme Court.

THE DISPATCH

Local: City files lawsuit over planned quarry, 3A

Food: Honey can serve as sugar substitute, 1C

KISS AT SCHOOL

Boy gets international attention

BY MARY TAWASNA
The Dispatch

One week ago, Jonathan Prevette was just another first-grader. This week, his face is being shown all over the world. The 6-year-old's newfound unexpected fame is a result of a simple kiss on the cheek. Or so he thought.

In reality, the kiss has turned out to be anything but simple.

Punished for what his mother Jackie, called "an innocent kiss," Jonathan has already appeared on CNN, the "Today Show," News, his family has received stop phone calls and TV network, Family Channel and from as far away as

THE KISSING BOY

SEE RELATED
EDITORIAL
ON PAGE 10A

Baby Boom

The rave reviews and rooftop ratings for her new syndicated talk show are very nice, but Rosie O'Donnell says the best thing to cross her desk is adopted son Parker Jaren (in July at 13 months). She's far from the only celeb now answering to the name Mama—others include Madonna, Roseanne, Melanie Griffith and Pamela Lee. "You fall in love instantly," O'Donnell says, recalling how she bonded with Parker at first blink. "I thought he was the most beautiful boy I'd ever seen."

ROSIE O'DONNELL AND PARKER

BORIS YELTSIN

He Keeps on Ticking

Boris Yeltsin, 65, came back twice from the dead this year: first to pull out a victory in Russia's July presidential election a few months after his approval ratings had dropped to single digits, and then to pull through a quintuple-bypass heart operation amid talk that his chances of recovery were no better than 50-50. Yeltsin's regime remained plagued by internal dissent, economic chaos and a humiliating defeat in Chechnya. But his resilience kept hope alive that Russia too would muddle through the tough transition to democracy.

Lost Innocents

It may take a village to raise a child but it only took one man to raze a village's hopes and dreams. Anguish and disbelief were etched upon the faces of tiny Dunblane, Scotland, after a deranged freelance photographer burst into a gym class at the local primary school and opened fire. Sixteen kindergartners and their teacher were killed and another 14 wounded before the gunman turned his weapon on himself. Only one child—5-year-old Robbie Hurst, who hid behind the body of his best friend during the massacre—escaped unharmed. "Lord knows how he will ever get over something like this," said his grandfather, Jackie Hurst.

Britons decried the fact that the shooter, Thomas Watt Hamilton, 43, was able to obtain a firearm permit, since he'd once brandished a gun against a mother who accused him of child molestation, a charge he'd faced on several earlier occasions. Both Queen Elizabeth and Prime Minister John Major made condolence calls to the town, and from around the world came stuffed animals and flowers. Some were tagged with one simple word: "WHY."

THE DUNBLANE TRAGEDY

Profiting on an Identity Crisis

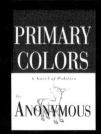

Never has an Anonymous become so well known. The undivulged identity of the author of *Primary Colors,* a bestselling roman à clef based on the 1992 Clinton election campaign, generated nearly as much dish as the scurrilous story line in which the George Stephanopoulos-style narrator has a fling with the candidate's Hillary-esque wife. Speculation on the identity of Anonymous ranged from Clinton adviser Stephanopoulos himself to cartoonist Garry Trudeau. When finally exposed, the author turned out to be *Newsweek* writer and CBS commentator Joe Klein, 49, who had repeatedly sworn his innocence with vehemence and indignation.

"In the end, he traded his journalistic credibility for 30 pieces of silver," scolded ex-White House press secretary Dee Dee Myers. Actually, the take, including film rights, was more like $6 million, and, along with the scorn and envy of colleagues, Klein wound up losing his CBS job but landing a possibly more prestigious columnist's berth on *The New Yorker.* Said the former Anonymous: "I feel relief and sadness."

JOE KLEIN

The Importance of Being Earnest

He went out with a bang—or the pop of a cork, anyway. The staff of Donahue's daytime talk show toasted their boss as he ended a remarkable 29-year run. With brows knit and heart on sleeve, the onetime Cleveland altar boy had quizzed everyone from Mandela to Marlo (interviewed her in 1977, tied the knot in 1980). Donahue, 60, brought audience participation to the talk show and adapted an old radio gambit, the phone-in ("Caller, are you there?"). He won 20 Emmys, but declining ratings for his stubbornly proper-minded show helped Donahue decide to unclip his mike.

DARKENED BY AIR TRAGEDY (TWA 800, A 7-YEAR-OLD PILOT), '96 WAS ALSO LIT BY HAPPY RETURNS (CLINTON, LUCID) AND SCRAPPY LANDINGS (STRUG)

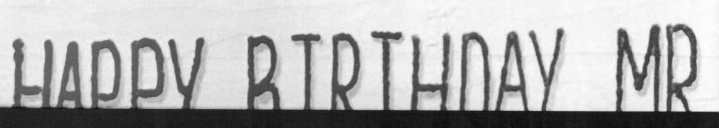

HAPPY BIRTHDAY MR

A New Lease

For the Clintons, it was another year of milestones

When the leader of the Free World celebrated his 50th birthday on August 18, an impressive (and eclectic) lineup of performers—including Tony Bennett, Jon Bon Jovi, Shania Twain and Whoopi Goldberg—showed up for a gala at Manhattan's Radio City Music Hall. But the show stealer was none other than Sister Mary Amaia, President Clinton's second-grade teacher, who admitted, "I was the one who gave little Bill a C in conduct." By 1996, her alumnus had shaped up a bit—or so thought the plurality (though not the majority) of voters on November 5, who made him the first Democrat to be reelected to the White House since Franklin Roosevelt.

The victory followed a race against Republican Senator Bob Dole that was memorable mostly for its dearth of memorable moments. The conventional wisdom was that voters had had it with negative campaigning. Instead, they got Pablum. "I happen to like the President," Dole said in an October 6 debate in Hartford. "I like Senator Dole," was Clinton's retort.

The year was more problematic for the First Lady, 49, beset on all sides by critics and pursued by a special prosecutor investigating her possible involvement with a series of scandals with ominous-sounding monikers—Filegate, Travelgate, Whitewater. But her book on children, *It Takes a Village,* was a bestseller and her own previously low-profile child, Chelsea, seemed to emerge in '96 as the picture of teenage poise and grace (if such qualities exist). The youngest Clinton had a milestone of her own, turning Sweet 16 and earning her driver's license. Asked once about her experience behind the wheel, she simply offered a warning: "Watch out if you come to D.C.!"

▲ The First Family shared a victory hug in Little Rock.

◄ Clinton's birthday bash put $10 million in campaign coffers.

27

▲ "Now people see him as the next President," Bay Buchanan, 47, declared of brother Pat, 58, after he stole the Massachusetts Republican primary (above). But his economic isolationism and anti-immigrant rants took his effort no further.

▼ After 1994's GOP landslide, strategist Dick Morris helped salvage the President's reelection hopes. But Morris's own fortunes sank when the *Star* exposed his affair with call girl Sherry Rowlands, who would eavesdrop as he advised Clinton. "He held the receiver between us and he was giggling and pointing for me to listen in," she said. "There was no doubt about it—it was the Man!" Morris, 48, out of a job, was driven home by wife Eileen McGann.

▲ "I'm not going to blow-dry my hair or change my part or something," said publishing heir Steve Forbes, 48, whose utter geekiness and flat-tax message resonated with voters enough to make him a surprise Republican contender. He lost but did nab one unlikely position: guest host of *Saturday Night Live.*

▲ "We're not articulate or whatever," Senator Bob Dole, 73, said at one point in his White House bid, "but we like to tell the truth, and we feel bad if we don't tell the truth." In 1996, the truth was that the Repubican nominee's campaign never really got off the ground. Hampered by a politically masterful incumbent, a solid economy, a lack of vision and his own peculiar version of the English language, the man from Russell, Kansas, found himself unable to bridge the gap. The campaign's high point was the convention speech by the other Dole—Elizabeth, who eschewed the podium to take an Oprah-style turn on the convention floor. It gave her husband a momentary boost in the polls— and also made her a contender to head the party's ticket in 2000.

➤ After a crazed gunman slew her husband and wounded her son in a 1994 New York commuter-train massacre, Carolyn McCarthy, 52, successfully lobbied Congress for an assault-weapons ban. Then the House—including Republican Dan Frisa, her representative—voted to repeal the bill. The nurse with no political experience was so mad she became a Democrat and ran against Frisa. And won. "Hopefully," she told the New York *Daily News*, "I'll stay the same person I am."

Lighting up Atlanta

Neither terror nor tackiness could spoil the Centennial Games

It was the most packaged Olympics in history. Thankfully, underneath the wrapping—the chauvinism of NBC's dice-and-splice heart-tugging and the welter of commercial sponsorships and corporate tents—the jewels sparkled: Decathlete Dan O'Brien brilliantly redeeming himself from his failure to make the Games in '92; Turkey's 4'11", 141-lb. Pocket Hercules, Naim Suleymanoglu, lifting 418¾ lbs. to beat (by five insurmountable pounds) his rival's world-record lift of a moment before; burly Matt Ghaffari of the U.S. sobbing uncontrollably after his silver in Greco-Roman wrestling; a band of American softball sisters embracing in a single bounding cluster after their win. While the packaging largely concealed from TV viewers occasional glitches in the IBM computer system and the woeful inadequacy of transportation, the lethal explosion of a pipe bomb in Centennial Park ripped the nation's psyche. Yet the Games still delivered magic and majesty.

It was a landmark year for U.S. women, who reaped the full harvest of Title IX, the 1972 federal law that upgraded ath-

◄ Carl Lewis, 35, soared into Olympic history with a long jump that won him a record-tying ninth gold medal. "This one," said Lewis, "is better than all the others."

letic funding for female athletes. Women captured 19 of the nation's 44 gold medals, with team sports like soccer, basketball and softball emerging as major magnets. The women themselves felt transformed. "I think we'll never be the same," says Dr. Dot Richardson, the shortstop who is also an orthopedic resident at USC Medical Center. "My cleats never touched the ground."

The unbroken spirit of Muhammad Ali, 54, shone through his Parkinsonism as he took the flame from swimmer Janet Evans and shakily lit the Olympic torch. On Day 16, the men's basketball team adoringly surrounded him as his missing 1960 gold medal was replaced.

Kerri Strug, 18, had "always been the bridesmaid," said '84 heroine Mary Lou Retton, until her near-perfect vault on a sprained ankle nailed the team gold for the U.S. women—and lifted her (in Coach Bela Karolyi's arms) into Olympic fable.

Amy Van Dyken, 23, teased in high school for being slow, said she won for "all the nerds out there." The 6' Colorado native also overcame asthma to become the first U.S. woman to win four golds in one Games—two in relays, plus the 50-freestyle and 100-butterfly. Her next splash was made on the cover of a Wheaties box.

▲ Michael Johnson's unprecedented sweep of the 200- and 400-meter golds surprised no one— but even Johnson said he was "shocked" by his world-record-smashing 19:32 in the 200.

➤ Lisa Leslie, the 6'5" center (and budding Wilhelmina model), put a victory squeeze on team-mate Jennifer Azzi after the American women dominated the hoops tourney wire to wire.

Justice Delayed

Exonerated Atlanta bombing suspect Richard Jewell indicts the media and FBI

"If my 15 minutes of fame was finding this package and saving some lives, that'll be fine with me," declared security guard Richard Jewell, 33. He was basking in media adulation after he had reported a suspicious knapsack and helped clear people away before a pipe bomb exploded, killing one, at Atlanta's Centennial Olympic Park. Two days later, the FBI confirmed a news report that Jewell was a suspect in the explosion—one who might plant a bomb and then "discover" it to win acclaim. The agency-released search warrant was full of defamatory innuendo, noting that Jewell "had no girlfriend . . . lives and breathes police stories." A media frenzy followed, with live broadcasts outside Jewell's apartment.

There was just one problem with the FBI's case: no evidence. Officially exonerated three long months later, Jewell indicted his tormentors. "In its rush to show the world how quickly it could get its man, the FBI trampled on my rights as a citizen," accused Jewell. "In its rush for the headline that the hero was the bomber, the media cared nothing for my feelings as a human being"—or, he might have added, for the presumption of innocence.

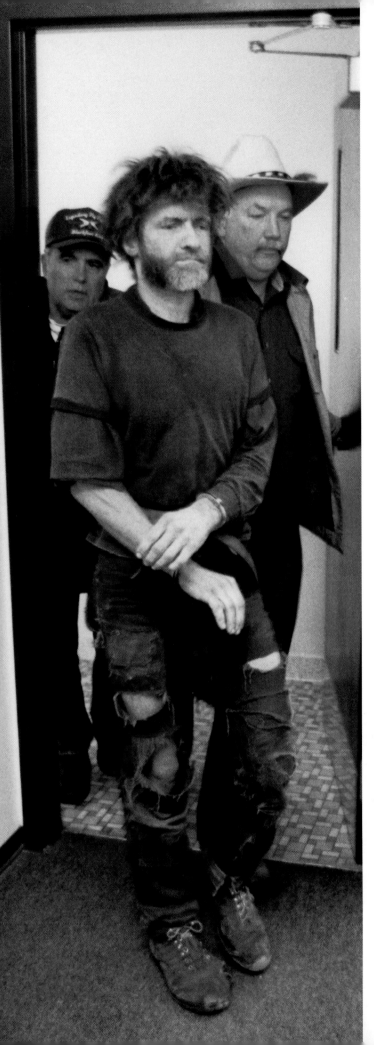

The Brothers Kaczynski

The sibling of the Unabomber suspect does the right thing

THIS IS A DOSTOYEVSKIAN TALE OF THE BROTHERS Kaczynski. They grew up in the comfortable Chicago suburb of Evergreen Park, sons of an outgoing engineer and a community-minded wife who founded a neighborhood preschool. Ted, the gifted older child, was a National Merit Scholarship finalist in high school and a member of the German, math and coin clubs. He was also a loner with a penchant for explosives who was once suspended from school when a paper container of chemicals he handed a female classmate blew up in her hands. On a fast academic track otherwise, Ted skipped two grades, graduated from Harvard, had his Ph.D. in math by 25 and landed an assistant professorship at Berkeley. But he was not a nurturing teacher: A published course review complained of his "completely ignoring the students." It had been the same in his undergraduate days. "We hardly knew him," says one-time roommate Patrick McIntosh. "He would go into his room, sit in his chair and rock."

In 1969, Ted resigned suddenly from the Berkeley faculty—perhaps overwhelmed by the political chaos engulfing the campus in the '60s. Two years later, he bought 1.4 acres of land outside the isolated mountain town of Lincoln, Montana, and eventually built a 10' x 12' plywood and tarpaper shack, which became his full-time

◄ Ted Kaczynski arrives at the Helena County courthouse hours after his arrest.

▲ "They were like night and day," said a neighbor of David (left) and Ted (center).

home. There, for 15 years, he read exotic books, spoke only when spoken to, did odd jobs such as selling tires at a truck stop and shot rabbits and squirrels for food

Ted's kid brother David was also a brilliant Ivy League alum, but he got his degree from Columbia in English. Far more sociable, he was an admired high school teacher for a couple of years in Lisbon, Iowa. Then, later, like his brother, David constructed his own small cabin, his in a remote area of West Texas. As a matter of fact, David had helped finance Ted's original land purchase in Montana. David was "a person who enjoyed his solitude but also enjoyed being around people," according to Father Mel LaFollette, a circuit Episcopal priest who met him in 1984. While Ted never seemed to have a girl-friend, David in 1990 married a woman he had corre-sponded with since high school. The couple settled in Schenectady, New York, she a philosophy professor at Union College and he a social worker at a halfway house counseling runaway kids.

Meanwhile, beginning in 1978 as the brothers took their divergent paths, a terrorist chillingly dubbed the Unabomber had been mailing handmade bombs that killed three people and maimed 23, most of the victims involved in science or computers. In late 1995, with a $1 million bounty and a 90-member federal task force on his trail, the Unabomber blackmailed *The Washington Post* and *The New York Times* into publishing a twisted, 35,000-word condemnation of industrial society.

A few months later, in early 1996, David Kaczynski, now 45, was helping his mother clean out the old family home and found boxes containing writings of Ted's that eerily resembled the anonymous manifesto. After ago-nized soul-searching, David contacted first a private investigator, and ultimately dealt with the FBI. When agents arrived at Ted's Montana shack, they found a live bomb, documents noting the names of Unabomber victims and notebooks crammed with drawings of explosive devices. With the arrest of Ted Kaczynski, 53, the FBI hoped to have ended the longest manhunt in its history.

⋀ Ted's cabin in snowy Montana had neither heat nor electricity.

➤ "They don't deserve this terrible mess," said a friend of David (at home) and wife.

Miracle in the Swamp

Taylor Touchstone, an autistic 10-year-old, survives four days lost in a morass of 'gators and snakes, but can't tell the tale

Naked, exhausted but, astoundingly, still treading water—that's how local boater Jimmy Potts found Taylor Touchstone, 14 miles from the spot on Florida's Turtle Creek where the boy disappeared while swimming with his family four days earlier. "I just pulled right up to him," says Potts. "You couldn't put a finger on that child without finding a scrape." While the boy's cuts and scratches have healed, doctors can't predict whether he'll remember the days he spent in the adjoining East Bay River Swamp, where 200 searchers tried to track him. Afflicted with moderate autism, a neurological disorder that impairs communication and reasoning, Taylor survived in an area where four Army Rangers died during a training exercise last year. His mother, Suzanne, believes the autism may have saved his life. Prone to focusing on a single detail, like a piece of string, for hours at a time, Taylor might have fixated so completely on one thing—his missing swimming trunks, for instance—that he blocked out fear and hunger. Autism experts concur. All the boy with a taste for Cheetos and video games could say was that he "saw lots of fish."

Her First Smile

Surgery helps Chelsey Thomas finally put on a happy face

"How come you can't smile?" other kids used to ask Chelsey Thomas, the little girl with almond-shaped blue eyes from Palmdale, California, who spent the first eight years of her life looking very glum indeed. Chelsey felt the same joys and sorrows other children do—you just couldn't see it. Born with a rare genetic defect called Moebius syndrome, she suffered from a variety of symptoms, including paralysis of her tongue and facial muscles. It was difficult for her to speak, chew, swallow, move her eyes or exhibit any facial expression, including a simple smile.

As a newborn, Chelsey was so weak from malnutrition and dehydration she almost died. But her mother, Lori, contrived a way to push a feeding tube down her baby's throat. "Once she started getting nutrition," Lori remembers, "she did really well." Defying doctors' predictions, Chelsey learned to both eat and talk. Lori founded a Moebius support group (now at 600 members) and, when Chelsey was 5, sought out Dr. Ronald Zuker of Toronto. Transplanting lengths of thigh muscle into the face, he had helped 30 patients like Chelsey. But the cost was prohibitive: $70,000 for each side of Chelsey's face. Luckily, the family's insurance company, Kaiser Permanante, covered it. Chelsey underwent two intricate 12-hour surgeries four months apart, each followed by a difficult recovery. Then it took a lot of practice. At first she had to bite down to get her smile to emerge. But she kept at it until it came naturally. "She has a great spirit," says teacher Kelly Merlo. "She was always excited to try something new." Today, Chelsey has plenty to grin about. "It's much better than I ever imagined it would be," says Lori. "It lights up her face."

Fire in the Sky

Flight 800 shattered many lives—and shook a nation

WHEN TWA FLIGHT 800, EN ROUTE TO PARIS FROM New York City's JFK International Airport, exploded 10 miles off the coast of Long Island on July 17 killing all 230 aboard, speculation flared almost as quickly as the fireball that engulfed the craft. Surely, terrorists did it—round up the usual Middle

Eastern suspects. As rumors spread on the Internet like a virus, there was the reflex assumption of a bomb planted aboard until eyewitness reports posited the alternative of a surface-to-air missile or, most disturbing, friendly fire from a U.S. naval exercise gone wrong. Traces of explosives were eventually detected, but they could have come from a recent drill that had been held on the plane to train bomb-sniffing dogs. By November when the salvage task force, air-safety investigators and FBI had recovered and sifted 95 percent of the wreckage, they began to doubt that criminal evidence would turn up, lending increasing credence to the possibility of a spark in the fuel tank caused by mechanical failure.

If the headline 230 DEAD was an abstraction, the nation was soon intimate with faces and stories behind that number: of Larkyn Lynn Dwyer, 11, a promising eques-

◄ Calverton, New York, was the assembly site for the remains of TWA 800.

▲ Crash victim Michel Breistroff's family and fiancée, Heidi Snow, say goodbye.

trian and violinist identified by a wad of spending money tucked into her sock at the last minute by her parents; Michel Breistroff, 25, a French-born Harvard grad en route to Germany to play pro hockey, who had phoned his girlfriend from JFK to propose marriage; Jacques and Connie Charbonnier, 65 and 49, a husband-and-wife flight-attendant team who had worked Flight 800 for 21 years; and Ruth and Edwin Brooks, 79 and 82, who had been happily traveling the world since his retirement two decades before. And there were, of course, the 16 teenagers and five chaperones of the Montoursville High School French Club, whose deaths devastated a Pennsylvania town of 5,000. As the Internet continued to crackle with conjecture about the crash, Robert Rupp, a Montoursville High senior not on the flight, created a web page of fond memories of the victims.

Dangerous Cargo

The ValuJet crash raises more safety fears

On May 11, ValuJet 592 lifted into clear skies over Miami. Minutes later, the passenger cabin filled with smoke and the plane disappeared into the Everglades, killing all 110 aboard. After salvage crews plumbed the muck (above), mystery gave way to agonizing knowledge: Improperly packed oxygen canisters apparently ignited the fire. ValuJet soon came under attack for lax supervision of subcontractors who handled the packaging, among other maintenance and repair tasks; so too did the Federal Aviation Administration, which had neglected to require smoke detectors in aircraft cargo bays.

Hitting Bottom

Robert Downey Jr. ends a streak of bizarre behavior in rehab, another casualty of Hollywood's heroin resurgence

Hollow-eyed and rail thin, he had begun to look, in the words of a neighbor, "a hundred years old." On July 29, sitting in court in a yellow prison jumpsuit, Robert Downey Jr. was asked if he appreciated the seriousness of his situation. "Yes," the 31-year-old actor said. "I do." Busted in June for speeding and the possession of coke and heroin and an unloaded .357 Magnum, the star of such films as *Chaplin* and *Restoration* posted bail. Three weeks later he stumbled into the home of neighbors in Malibu, stripped and passed out in the bed of their 11-year-old son. The court ordered him into detox but within days he'd escaped to a friend's house. Security guards apprehended him, and this time he went to jail for having left the court-ordered program. For Downey, who first entered treatment in 1988, drugs are almost lifelong companions. (He and his father, film director Robert Sr., would bond by getting high together, Downey has said of his youth.) Downey is only one of several show-business luminaries to tangle with heroin this year. In July, Jonathan Melvoin, a keyboardist for Smashing Pumpkins, died of an overdose. (The band fired drummer Jimmy Chamberlin, who had done heroin with Melvoin that night.) Scott Weiland, lead singer of Stone Temple Pilots, also entered rehab this year—twice. Downey has since been sentenced to three years' probation and an extended commitment to a drug recovery program.

Balance Point

After a steep slide into manic depression, Margot Kidder finds her way home

Playing Superman's girlfriend, she once flew to the North Pole with the Man of Steel. But last spring, when actress Margot Kidder was found—disheveled, dirty and missing the caps of her front teeth—in a backyard in a Los Angeles suburb, her high-altitude Hollywood life seemed farther away than the planet Krypton. "You may not believe me," she said to Elaine Lamb, owner of the yard she'd wandered into, "but I'm Margot Kidder." Lamb called 911, and soon the actress was telling her story to police, who had been searching for her for days. Tales followed of time spent in a homeless man's cardboard box, a near-rape and the delusion that she was stalked by assassins hired by her first husband and father of her daughter Maggie, author Thomas McGuane. "I was like one of those ladies you see talking to the space aliens on the street corner," she says.

Kidder, 47, now recognizes that the root of most of her problems—including "mood swings that could knock over a building"—is manic depression, a disease that causes those afflicted to vacillate between euphoric highs and desperate, often suicidal, lows. Though Kidder had suffered bouts since adolescence—she tried to kill herself at 14 when a boyfriend left her—she was not diagnosed until eight years ago. Even then she did not accept the diagnosis (or take the prescribed lithium) until after her most recent descent. The disease grew even more dangerous when a 1990 car accident left Kidder partly paralyzed and greatly in debt, leading her to repeatedly anesthetize herself with alcohol and drugs.

Just two weeks before finding herself a street person, Kidder had been working on her memoirs, aptly titled *Calamities*. She had entered, as she did every two years or so, a state of blazing creative ferment. "It's very hard to convince a manic person that there is anything wrong," says Kidder. "You have no desire to sleep. You are full of ideas." When a computer virus swallowed files on her laptop, causing three years of work to vanish in a few days, Kidder was driven, she says, to "absolute delusion." Paranoia is common in the manic phase of her disease, and Kidder imagined agents and assassins everywhere.

Now she has bounced back. For the first time, she has fully acknowledged her condition and is taking her lithium—though she still mistrusts the drug—and is also trying acupuncture and newer drugs as well as Native American remedies. She is back at work on her memoirs, after a computer whiz retrieved most of the lost files. More important, she has transformed a relationship with daughter Maggie Kirn, 21, that was once, she says, "a bottomless well of grief." "Margot is incredibly strong," says brother John Kidder, who has helped her get back on her feet. "She is a survivor."

Lesson Aloft

Spunky Jessica Dubroff died pursuing a dream. But was it hers or her parents'?

THE 7-YEAR-OLD GIRL WHOSE BODY LAY IN A CASKET topped with a model airplane "had a full, wonderful, exquisite life," said her mother, "and she died in a state of joy." An admiring neighbor said that Jessica "was encouraged to do whatever she wanted—to reach for the stars." A modern-day Icarus, Jessica Dubroff had many Americans wondering whether the lives they had carved for themselves and their children were too earthbound. Then, like the child of Greek myth given fragile wings by his father, Jessica plummeted, crashing into a residential neighborhood in Cheyenne, Wyoming, moments after taking off on the second leg of her quest to be the youngest

Schooled entirely at home by her idiosyncratic mother, Lisa Hathaway, 41, Jessica and her brother Joshua, 9, were not allowed to read children's books, watch TV at home or play with toys. They socialized with adults. Vegetarians, they snacked on red bell peppers—never candy. "They're working kids," said former neighbor Ruth Hart. "If I was pulling weeds, they'd come and pull weeds with me. Sometimes they'd just sit on the porch with me and chat. It was just like talking to adults."

Similarly drawn to Jessica was Joe Reid, a stockbroker who gave flying lessons out of Half Moon Bay, near Hathaway's rented house in rural Pescadero, California. Four months before Jessica's ill-fated flight, Hathaway had approached Reid and said her children wanted to learn to fly. Reid, a deeply religious Vietnam vet, was "a total contrast" to the dream-dealing entrepreneur Dubroff and New Ager Hathaway, says George Auld, part owner with Reid of the single-engine Cessna that crashed. Yet he bonded with Jessica, his youngest pupil ever. "They both loved flying and had a love of life and people," says Auld. "It was amazing when you watched them together. Joe was always happy and smiles."

Was the venture irresponsible? Apparently Reid did not think so; he "just figured he would be there always on the right seat like a prolonged lesson," says his wife Ana. Ironically, the adults in Jessica's life may have failed her not by giving her too much responsibility but by failing to handle their own roles prudently. There is evidence that Jessica's plane was too heavily laden to take off safely at Cheyenne's high altitude and that the weather that day, which included wind, sleet and thunderstorms, was too rough for small aircraft. What was the rush?

Hathaway, for one, though deeply grieved, was unregretful. "If children could not do anything unsafe, they wouldn't go anywhere," she said. Praise or blame notwithstanding, the nation was left to mourn that Jessica had gone too far, too soon.

▼ **Lloyd Dubroff looked skyward with Jessica on the day of the doomed takeoff.**

▼ **A friend consoled Mom Lisa Hathaway before the funeral procession.**

pilot ever to traverse the U.S. The crash instantly killed Jessica, her father, Lloyd, 57, and instructor Joe Reid, 52.

In the aftermath of the crash, many felt that Jessica's parents had overreached in their bid to provide their children with empowering experiences. Some accused Lloyd Dubroff—who had faxed notice of Jessica's impending flight to the *Guinness Book of World Records*—of pursuing a publicity stunt that exploited his daughter. Others, especially those close to the family, argue that though her parents hadn't lived together since 1990, both were deeply committed to their children's welfare, and had raised a remarkable brood.

Pulp Friction

Joan Collins goes to court to defend her right to write badly

There is a difference between a good trashy novel and just plain trash. At least that's what Random House maintained in rejecting a manuscript by actress Joan Collins, demanding the return of a $1.3-million advance. Editor Joni Evans said Collins, 62, had submitted drafts that were "over the top, dated [and] melodramatic." The former *Dynasty* star—sister of good-trashy novelist Jackie—sued. Her lawyer argued, in effect, that as long as the manuscript was in English and didn't defame anyone, Collins had fulfilled her part of the deal and the publisher had to pay up. The jurors saw it her way, and she got to keep $1.2 million of her advance.

Life on Mars

It's no revelation to the folks in this Pennsylvania burg

When NASA scientists announced that a meteorite, found in Antarctica and previously identified as Martian, contained fossils of microscopic organisms—the first sign ever of life beyond our planet —the 1,700 residents of Mars, Pennsylvania, thought the news anything but alien. The earthly Martians boast their own 2,800-lb. steel flying-saucer sculpture in the town square; a bank that offers "service out of this world"; a football team dubbed the Planets; and license plates that read, WELCOME TO MARS: JUST A LITTLE CLOSER TO HEAVEN.

Time Traveler

The 500-year-old Incan "Ice Maiden" reveals it was never easy being teen

She's a study in contradictions: ancient, yet only 13 years old; preserved in ice atop Peru's Mount Ampato, yet a hot new attraction for tourists at the National Geographic Society's Explorer's Hall in Washington, D.C.; world famous, yet anonymous. The Incan girl known simply as the Ice Maiden— found by American anthropologist Johan Reinhard, 52, while mountain climbing—may reveal more information than any other pre-Columbian discovery. Her remains include strong teeth and bones (indicating good nutrition) as well as intact organs, tissues and unfragmented DNA. But she also tells a frightening tale. It is thought she was sacrificed as a gift to the sacred mountain, her skull smashed by a blow from a priest. Being chosen to die in this way was considered a high honor, and the Ice Maiden probably submitted willingly, dispatched to the next world with an entourage of gold figurines.

Flames of Hatred

A disturbing, unsolved wave of arsons consumes black churches in the South

WHEN WILLIE CARTER WAS A little boy, his father carried him every Sunday morning up a wooded hill on the outskirts of Boligee (pop. 300), Alabama, to the Little Zion Baptist Church, a tiny African-American congregation. Years later, when he and his wife, Leola, had seven kids of their own, Carter spent Saturday evenings laying out the children's Sunday best, shining their shoes so that the whole family would be ready to troop off to Little Zion in the morning. "I couldn't find no better place than church," says Carter, 58, a minister who works in construction. "It kept me alive."

So he was stunned by the telephone call he received late on the evening of January 11. "Y'all's church is on fire!" the caller said. But even before fire trucks could be called, the red-brick, tin-steepled structure had collapsed. The next morning, surveying the heap of ash, Carter "felt like somebody hit me with something," he says. "I couldn't believe it." The church's 40 members puzzled over whether faulty wiring or a gas leak might have caused the blaze—until they heard that Mt. Zoar Baptist Church, serving a black congregation four miles away, had burned down the same night. "Then," says Carter, "I thought, 'Something's going on here.' "

Boligee's white mayor, Buddy Lavender—who is also police chief and fire chief of the poor, mainly black community—agrees. The arsonist, he says, "is a racist, pure and simple." After all, the two fires occurred the day the *Greene County Democrat* reported the sentencing of two young white men who had vandalized three black churches in a neighboring coun-

ty in February 1994. There has been speculation that the arsonist was reacting to that verdict.

In less than three years, fires have damaged or destroyed at least 25 black churches in the South. Authorities say the wave began on the 25th anniversary of Martin Luther King's assassination— April 4, 1993—when three white teenagers, using hymnals and artificial flowers as kindling, burned down two black churches near McComb, Mississippi.

Many of these burnings remain unsolved, FBI officials say. "They're putting a dagger into the heart of the black community," says Mary Frances Berry, who heads the U.S. Commission on Civil Rights. "In symbolic terms there isn't anything worse that anyone could do."

FBI and ATF investigators stress that they have not uncovered a co-ordinated campaign of destruction. Yet many observers say the fires are symptomatic of a time of political scapegoating and rising racial tension. "I think much of the country is in a state of denial when it comes to race relations," says Bobby Doctor of the civil rights commission's southern regional office. "We've not solved this problem."

As with so many racially charged issues, the solution has been complicated by a battle of perceptions. The liberal National Council of Churches, a leader in rebuilding efforts, has been accused by a conservative Protestant group of perpetuating a "great church-fire hoax" to "promote its racial agenda." Other conservative groups have pointed out that as many white churches as black have been burned—to which the NCC coun-

Caught up in the conflagration was the Boligee, Alabama, church of 92-year-old pastor W. D. Lewis.

ters that there are more white churches than black in the U.S. And Deval Patrick, head of the Justice Department's civil rights division and cochairman of an FBI/ATF task force devoted to church arson, says that two-thirds of the 30 incidents in which arrests have recently been made were racially motivated.

Some Americans are fighting the madness. When arsonists destroyed the Inner City Church in Knoxville, Tennessee, where Green Bay Packers defensive lineman Reggie White is assistant pastor, more than $300,000 in donations flooded in—much of it from white football fans who have heard of the church's plight. In Madison, Georgia, where a teen gang destroyed the historic Springfield Baptist Church, white supporters have donated more than $30,000 toward the half-million dollars it will take to replace the church. There are also signs, however, of renewed tolerance of racism. In the spring of 1996, Klan member John Howard opened the Redneck Shop in Laurens, South Carolina, a store peddling KKK-embossed clothing and Confederate memorabilia. And for many African-Americans, the arsonists' message has spoken louder than attempts at redress. The charred remains of the churches have raised painful memories of the 1960s civil rights struggle, when hundreds of black churches were vandalized and burned. "The people who burned down churches in the '50s and '60s are still alive today," says White. "This is going to keep going until we as Americans stand up against them."

Dead Man Waking

Left for dead on Everest, Beck Weathers revived in time to make the long trip home

"I remember the voices getting dim, faint, far away," says Seaborn Beck Weathers of the moment before he lost consciousness in the sudden blizzard that hit Mount Everest just as 150 climbers were aiming for its 29,028-foot peak. Canadian climber Stuart Hutchinson, finding Weathers half covered in fresh snow, unburied him and broke ice chunks off his face—and reported him dead. Word was relayed to Weathers's wife, Peach, 47, who wondered how she would break the news to her sleeping children, Beck II, 17, and Meg, 14.

Eight climbers from three continents died on Everest that day, May 10. The fallen included Weathers's expedition leader, Rob Hall, 36, who, exhausted and without oxygen after trying in vain to save another team member, managed to make a final radio call home from Everest to his pregnant wife in New Zealand. His last words were "don't worry about me too much."

But the news of Weathers's demise proved quite premature. The 49-year-old Dallas pathologist, who had begun climbing 10 years earlier because he "thought it would be interesting to face" his fear of heights, awoke after a full night on the mountain to find himself lying in the snow, his face once again sheeted with ice and his right hand frozen "like a rock." Gradually grasping his situation, he began thinking about his wife and children —"the things I wouldn't be able to say to them"—and found the strength to climb to his feet. Staggering, nearly blind, Weathers eventually, miraculously, found the blue tents of the camp from which he had embarked as part of an eight-person team two days before. The astonished climbers cut the frozen clothes from his body, gave him oxygen and warmed him with a hot-water bottle. Back in Dallas, three hours after hearing that her husband had perished, Peach Weathers received a blissful follow-up: Beck was in critical condition—but alive.

Ahead of him still lay a two-day trek to the lower camp, 11,000 feet below the summit; a perilous helicopter rescue in high winds and thin air; the near-certain loss of his right hand and probably part of his left (his face, blackened by frostbite, is expected to heal with only minor scarring). It's all a small price to pay, Weathers says. "All those things I worried I'd never get the chance to say to my wife and kids— I've had the opportunity to say."

Weathers's wife, Peach, and their two children (center and right) welcomed him home when he arrived at the Dallas-Fort Worth Airport last May.

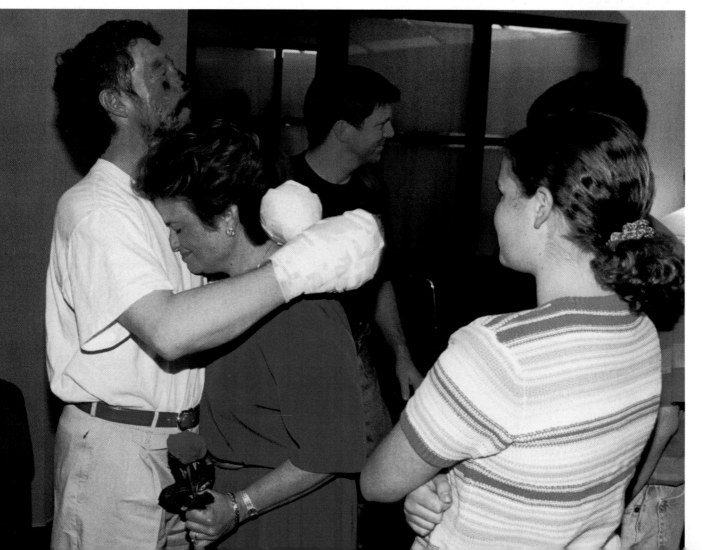

A Mom's a Mom

Binti Jua shows mother love heroically transcends species

"The gorilla's got my baby!" a Brookfield, Illinois, woman cried in horror as the crowd around her gasped. But their fear soon turned to awe and gratitude. When the woman's 3-year-old boy fell 24 feet onto the cement floor of the primate pavilion at the Brookfield Zoo, a 160-pound western lowland gorilla named Binti Jua rushed over and scooped him up. She rocked the unconscious lad in her arms, kept other apes at bay and carried him to the compound's entrance, where zoo staffers and paramedics were standing by. "I could not believe how gentle she was," said Celeste Lombardi, a director at Ohio's Columbus Zoo, who had raised Binti for the first month of her life. "I was very proud." The child—whose parents have requested anonymity—suffered a broken hand, abrasions and minor bruising to the brain, but was home in less than a week.

Born at Columbus Zoo in March 1988, Binti Jua (Swahili for Daughter of Sunshine) was raised by humans because her mother, Lulu, did not have enough milk. When Binti became pregnant at 6, her trainers, concerned that she had no strong maternal role model, gave her "mothering lessons." Using a woolly stuffed doll, they taught Binti to nurse and carry her baby constantly as gorillas do in the wild. Her daughter Koola was born in February 1995, and Binti proved a natural.

A few rungs up the evolutionary ladder, Binti would have had a guest spot on Letterman, but instead, her life was completely unaffected by her heroic act. She seemed perfectly content to spend her days lounging on the limbs of her favorite tree, grooming Koola, who had bounced along during the rescue, clinging to her mother.

"She probably saved his life from the other gorillas," says paramedic **Bill Lambert,** who was visiting the zoo with his family and caught the rescue on videotape (right). Above, Binti Jua, one great ape, cools out with daughter Koola.

Gifford's Labor Pains

Kathie Lee, a marquee label in marketing, is shamed into becoming a force for reform

A preternaturally perky talk show host was quaking with unaccustomed indignation and rage. "You can say I'm ugly, you can say I'm not talented," blurted a teary Kathie Lee Gifford to millions tuned in to *Live with Regis and Kathie Lee* last spring, "but when you say that I don't care about children . . . how dare you!" Her emotional outburst followed a charge that some articles of her Kathie Lee clothing line were manufactured by exploited child laborers in a seamy Honduran factory. Her accuser was the National Labor Committee, a human-rights monitoring group. "You'd swear you're at a high school," testified NLC executive director Charles Kernaghan to a congressional committee investigating the problem. "But you're in these factories where they work 14-hour shifts."

At first, Gifford, 42, pleaded ignorance of any violations and noted that $1 million of her $9-million profit the previous year had been donated to the Association to Benefit Children, a charity that opened two New York City shelters for crack-addicted babies. But when the sordid circumstances at her operations kept surfacing and the furor continued, she promised to create a watchdog organization to correct labor infractions in the 25 plants turning out her Wal-Mart line. Kathie Lee had become the leading label in the celeb clothing field, with a stunning $300-million volume in its first year, and other name marketeers quickly joined her push for labor reform. Soap star Deidre *(Days of Our Lives)* Hall immediately began checking out the Providence factories producing her costume jewelry peddled on the Home Shopping Network. And diet guru Richard Simmons boasted that even before the Gifford exposé he had personally inspected the international factories churning out his 17 licensed products. "Every bit of embroidery, every button, every pleat, I have to know about it," he said. Problems turned up at home as well as overseas. "Sweatshops are returning to America," warned Labor Secretary Robert B. Reich, noting that at least half of the domestic cutting and sewing shops were paying under the minimum wage and that one-third subjected workers to health and safety hazards.

Indeed, shortly after the original complaint about Gifford's operation in Honduras, it was reported that Seo Fashions, a New York City supplier of Kathie Lee garments, had cheated 25 men and women out of up to four weeks pay just after they had finished a rush order for 50,000 blouses. At that point, Kathie Lee's husband, ABC sportscaster Frank Gifford, personally visited the garment-district factory. He found a bleak sweatshop, dimly lit except for the glare of a dozen TV news teams. "Everything is dirty," said an undocumented, Mexican-born seamstress. "The trash isn't picked up, and the two bathrooms aren't fit for pigs." Appalled, the former football star proceeded to hand out $300 apiece to the workers. "These people were in dire straits," said Kathie Lee. "We had to do something to help." Added Frank: "I apologize for our country."

◄ Gifford, dressed in an ensemble from her signature line, at first went on the defensive on her own show.

▲ Workers like these at a New York City sweatshop toil 10 hours a day for less than the minimum wage.

He Wants to Tell You

Acquitted but not forgiven, a lonely O.J. fights
in court and in the court of public opinion

The folks at Hertz did not come begging for their old
pitchman's services in 1996. O.J. Simpson spent most of
the year holed up in his Rockingham estate, brooding
over legal and financial problems. His court battle to
clear himself in the June 1994 murder of his wife Nicole
and Ron Goldman had left him virtually broke with an
image so tattered he had little prospect for future
income. Worse, perhaps, he found himself shunned by
the entertainment community and unwelcome even at
old haunts like the Riviera Country Club, where he once
spent much of his time on the links.

Seeking an escape, he turned up in May in England, in
the unlikeliest of places: the Oxford Union Society's debat-
ing hall, where more than 900 students showed up for a
question-and-answer session. So pleased was he with his
72-minute performance that when told time was running
out, he groused playfully, "I've got a lot more to say."

Much of it he said in a $29.95 video in which Simpson
told his side of the events surrounding the murders. It
sold poorly—in part because no mainstream network
would run Simpson's advertisements. Or maybe because
the market was so utterly saturated with various ver-
sions of the story: Almost monthly in 1996 another
blockbuster book on the case would hit bestseller lists.

None of them could claim to be the last word. In
September, Simpson was back in court, facing a wrong-
ful death civil suit brought by the families of the victims. This time a new witness would join the familiar
parade: Simpson himself, who under oath denied com-
mitting the murders or ever even striking Nicole. But
he was forced to admit he could not explain how his
blood turned up on Nicole's gate or Nicole's and Ron's
in his Bronco. "I wish," he said at another point in his
testimony, "I were anywhere but here."

Judge Hiroshi Fujisaki barred cameras from the court-
room, but the enterprising E! network tried to assuage
public craving by airing nightly trial excerpts, stiffly performed by a cast of lookalike actors, some of whom took
the job to heart. "Everything in my body tells me, 'The
whole world is against you. Everybody thinks you're a
murderer,' " said Stephen Wayne Eskridge, the former
jazz musician who played Simpson. "Man, even though
I'm just acting, that's a lot to carry around."

Capital Punishment

Don Imus roasts, and is singed, in D.C.

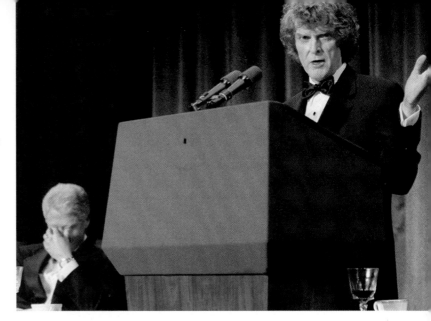

Washington was shocked, *shocked*, but Don Imus, 54, was unrepentant after skewering both Clintons, and other politicos, at the annual gala of the Radio and Television Correspondent's Association. References to the President's womanizing and the First Lady's Whitewater involvement were "way, way, way over the line," said ABC's Cokie Roberts, and the White House tried (in vain) to kill a C-SPAN rebroadcast. Asked if he would apologize, the I-Man snapped, "I don't *think* so! I let 'em off the hook!"

In the Paint

For hoops star Dennis Rodman flamboyance is anything but a drag

Dennis Rodman's August announcement that he would marry in public in Manhattan the next day prompted an intriguing speculation: What kind of girl would the neon-haired, tattoo-embroidered, lipstick-wearing, rebound-snaring, 6'8" Chicago Bulls forward go for? Why, one just like Dennis Rodman—as became obvious on the appointed day when a rather tall and well-muscled figure in a bridal gown (left) alighted from a horse-drawn carriage on Fifth Avenue and strolled right into a bookstore. Lo and behold, inside were stacks of Rodman's new bestselling autobiography, *Bad as I Wanna Be*, and a line of fans just itching to get his signature inside the cover and fork over their $22.95 a copy.

Touting cross-dressing as a form of therapy (for shyness and inner conflict) and tossing up gossipy three-pointers (former lover Madonna "wasn't an acrobat, but . . . wasn't a dead fish, either"), the 35-year-old author showed that he is as fiendishly brilliant at grabbing attention as he is at hauling in errant basketballs. His next project: "A guide to living," titled *Rodman Rules*.

The High Life

After her record, 188-day space odyssey, astronaut Shannon Lucid can't wait for Mars

She once said she became an astronaut because it was the only way to get closer to God than her father did in his calling as a tent and radio evangelist. There were times, however, during her six-month voyage aboard the Russian space station *Mir*—history's longest mission by an American—when Shannon Lucid had had it with the heavens and her two craftmates named Yuri. "It's like living in a camper in the back of your pickup with your kids," she said, "when it's raining and no one can get out." Her sole other complaint was over the shortage of potato chips, other junk food and, worst, when *Mir* ran out of M&M's.

A four-trip shuttle veteran, Lucid, 53, wrote an eighth-grade essay voicing her dream of becoming a rocket scientist only to have her teacher scoff at such a possibility for a girl. But Lucid, born while her parents were missionaries in China and weaned in a Japanese prison camp, paid no heed, going on to fly her own rickety Piper Clipper and eventually earning a doctorate in chemistry from the University of Oklahoma. In 1978, she became one of NASA's original six woman astronauts, along with Sally Ride—and Judith Resnik, who would die in the 1986 *Challenger* tragedy.

During her 67,454,841-mile tour, Lucid conducted myriad scientific experiments and gave English lessons to her cosmonaut fellow travelers. She confessed to enjoying the respite from housework and grocery shopping for her earth family back in suburban Houston— husband Mike, an oil-company executive, and their three children, 20 to 27. But she communicated with them daily via e-mail on a Russian laptop and biweekly on video feeds. She also screened films including *Apollo 13;* read histories of the American West and finally finished *David Copperfield*; and spent hours a day on a stationary bike and treadmill. When she returned to earth after 188 days, Lucid was proud to walk out on her own two feet and said she couldn't wait to orbit again, ideally on the first jaunt to Mars. She was met by NASA administrator Daniel Goldin, who brought her a huge gold-wrapped gift box from the Commander in Chief. The Clintons had sent her a fresh supply of M&M's.

Solo on Ice

After the death of her husband and soulmate, Ekaterina Gordeeva bravely skates again

Lying on their sides in a closet in Simsbury, Connecticut, are a pair of ice skates that will never be used again. Like the piles of clothes, dog-eared books and a calling card that lies on the kitchen counter, they are household shrines to the idyllic time before the sudden death of their owner, Russian skater Sergei Grinkov, in November 1995. "I have left everything just the way it was," says Ekaterina Gordeeva, 25, the wispy, 5'2" skater, who was Grinkov's partner on ice and in life for 13 years and his wife for five. "I can't touch anything."

The tale of Gordeeva and Grinkov, paired when they were 11 and 15 by coaches in Moscow, is a story of love, loss, unfathomable grief—and healing. Fellow skaters remember seeing the pair sneak kisses on a Soviet team bus. "We always thought of them as so lucky," remembers Elena Bechke, a 1992 Russian silver medalist.

In *My Sergei: A Love Story,* published last November, Gordeeva told the story of their relationship, their two Olympic gold medals, the birth of their daughter, Daria, and Grinkov's sudden death at 28 during a practice session, a victim of undiagnosed heart disease. Last February, in Hartford, Gordeeva skated sans Grinkov for the first time, her performance a beautiful ice poem commemorating their love. Her greatest solace now is not skating but Daria, 3, who has her father's fetching smile and kind eyes. "I need her around me," Gordeeva says. "She brings me back to reality."

▼ Gordeeva
scooped up Daria
last February after
concluding her first
performance since
Grinkov's death.

Emotional Slam

Pete Sampras rebounds from his worst loss: the death of his coach

It was a match made in heaven—the coupling of a shy, brooding, tennis natural, Pete Sampras, with the game's gregarious, master teacher, Tim Gullikson. Though before they linked up, Sampras had won the 1990 U.S. Open at 19, the youngest men's champion in the history of the event, he sensed that he lacked the temperament and work ethic to fully exploit his god-given potential. "I didn't have a great attitude," Sampras reflects. "I had some talent, but I was a bit . . . flaky might be the word." Fifteen months later, he hired Gullikson, a 19-years-older tour journeyman, best known for winning doubles titles with his identical twin, Tom, before he found his calling as a coach, mentoring greats like Martina Navratilova. "Within a few months we were comfortable around each other," recalls Sampras. "It was much more than a player-coach relationship. He was my best buddy. He brought a little personality out of me off court."

On court, it didn't work so bad either as Sampras won another four Grand Slam titles, including three consecutive Wimbledons. But, suddenly in 1995, after a period of illness, Gullikson was diagnosed with oligodendroglioma, a rare brain cancer. Sampras, belying his machinelike public image, broke down and sobbed during the quarterfinals of the '95 Australian Open, and Gullikson did most of his tutoring via television and phone. Last May, he died at 44. Sampras, attending the first funeral of his life, started to give a eulogy but couldn't finish. "Tennis is a great game, but . . . it's not the most important thing in life," he said later. "It kind of put everything into perspective." He worked with Tim's brother to raise funds for cancer research and treatment, and returned to the circuit but was unable to win another Slam until the '96 U.S. Open, when he dramatically blew out Michael Chang in straight sets. But, as Sampras has said, "I don't think I'll ever get over Tim's death."

Sampras dedicated his trophy at the '96 U.S. Open to Gullikson (with him above in 1995).

Oscar Worthy

Christopher Reeve wins Hollywood's heart

"It felt like a homecoming," said Oscar-night surprise guest Christopher Reeve, after a surge of applause in his honor shook the Dorothy Chandler Pavilion. Reeve, 43, paralyzed from the neck down in a 1995 equestrian accident, radiated a beatific strength as he adjured the rapt audience to "take risks" and "tackle social issues." It was the outset of a remarkable year for the actor, who made his directorial debut with the HBO drama *In the Gloaming,* addressed the Democratic National Convention, lobbied for paralysis research and stuck to a grueling rehab. Throughout, he credited his Man of Steel optimism to wife Dana Morosini. "She has never once wavered," he said. "I feel I owe her my life."

A ROSIE BY ANY OTHER NAME WOULD STILL BE HOT
(BUT A McCONAUGHEY MIGHT BE EASIER TO PRONOUNCE).
DO NOT ATTEMPT TO ADJUST YOUR MORISSETTE!

SENSATIONS

Best Actress winner Susan Sarandon greets Reeve and Morosini at the post-Oscar Governors Ball (left: Robin Williams in crisscross specs)

▲ **MEL GIBSON** brandished his Best Picture and Best Director Oscars for *Braveheart*. No longer the boozer and carouser of *Mad Max* years, Gibson, at 40, has become a consummate husband and father (of six)—and a megastar who was paid $20 million for *Ransom*.

Monge (left) and Ruiz spawned a worldwide hit.

Macarena Madness

A party perennial is born

Unplug the Electric Slide, hang up the Hora. A new dance craze took America by the hips this year. After a summer ruling the *Billboard* singles charts, the Macarena—a kind of PG-13 Hokey Pokey—is requested on cruise ships more often than Dramamine. It first got under foot in 1993, when the Spanish duo Los del Rio wrote a song about a lovesick temptress named Macarena and improvised the dance steps at a concert. Soon Europeans were Maca-rocking madly, and in 1995 a deejay began spinning the disc in a Miami nightclub. "Every time I played it," remembers Johnny Caride, 30, "everyone went crazy." Caride's band, the Bayside Boys, licensed the song and remixed it in English. The U.S. women gymnasts danced a Macarena after their Olympic team triumph. A Macarena Night was held at Yankee Stadium in August.

Now it's pinch-me time for Antonio Romero Monge and Rafael Ruiz, aka Los del Rio, childhood chums from Seville. Both 48, with four kids apiece, they had barely earned macaroon money in 34 years in pop music. "We thought Macarena would create a force," says Monge. Grandmas will be doing it at weddings for years to come.

Manic Martial Plan

Hong Kong's action hero Jackie Chan takes his real-deal stunts Stateside

He's jumped from a flying plane to a hot-air balloon and roller-skated beneath a speeding truck. But in his 43 movies there is one stunt Jackie Chan, 41, had never accomplished: a big U.S. hit. That all changed when the martial-arts wizard with the slapstick sensibility produced his first film with major Hollywood distribution. *Rumble in The Bronx* grossed over $30 million and was critically praised. On its heels Miramax re-released earlier Chan flicks *Crime Story* and *Drunken Master II*. Chan's parents, an embassy cook and maid, left him behind in Hong Kong at 7 when they moved to Australia and he plunged into studies of martial arts and singing at the Chinese Opera Institute to assuage loneliness. By 17 his success had sparked a local movie boom. "He is one of the greatest physical comedians since sound came into films," said Quentin Tarantino, presenting Chan with a 1996 MTV movie award. "If I could be any actor, I would have the life Jackie Chan has."

1. Thrust your right hand out, palm down, then your left hand out, palm down.

2. After both arms are extended, turn palms up, first right, then left. With us?

3. Right hand crosses body to left shoulder, and left crosses to right shoulder.

4. Put right hand to right ear, left hand to left ear. Hands then cross to hips.

5. Hands on hips, uncrossed, shake your booty. Jump and clap, turning 90 degrees.

59

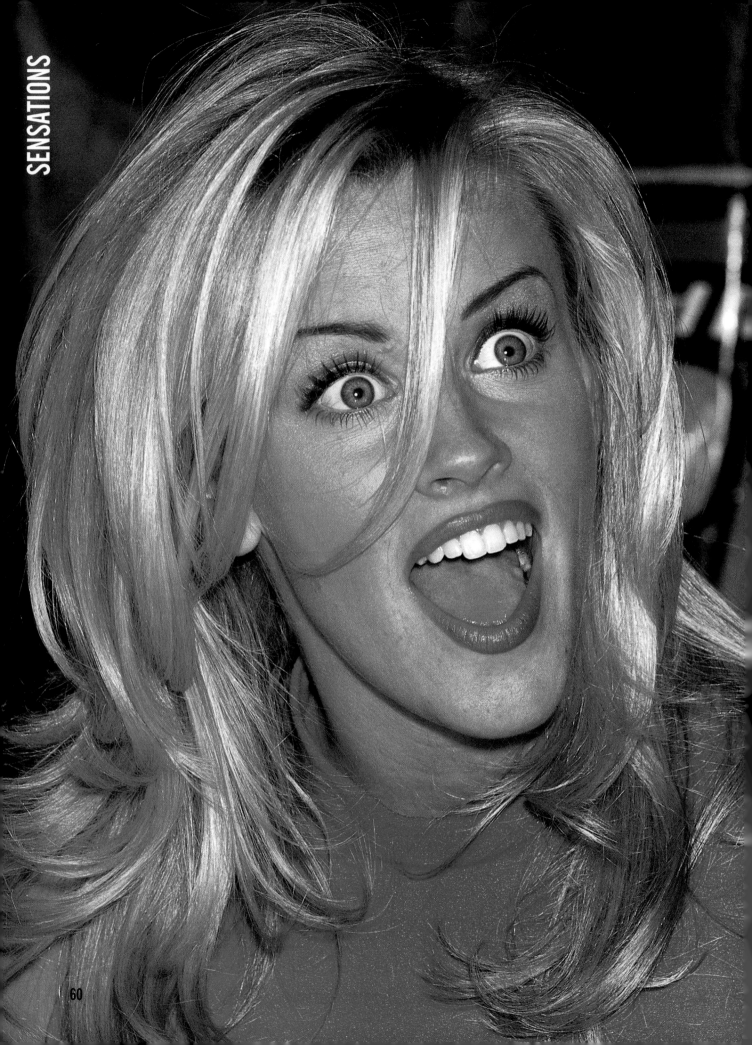

Two High-Volt Gen Xers Seize The Spotlight

Fans ate up the big Mcs of 1996, MTV's Jenny McCarthy and actor Matthew McConaughey

He projects "intelligence and integrity" tinged with "a bit of the bad boy," says director Joel Schumacher. She radiates sexual energy with a winning wisp of the good girl. He, Matthew McConaughey, 26, the smoldering lawyer lead in the movie of John Grisham's *A Time to Kill,* has been compared to Paul Newman ("the next") and Marlon Brando ("the early"). She, Jenny

McConaughey fights the flames of hatred in *A Time to Kill*.

McCarthy and McConaughey

McCarthy, 23, hostess of MTV's mosh-pit dating game *Singled Out,* has been compared to Vanna White on a sugar high (she feasts on Cap'n Crunch and kick-boxes off the excess cals).

A working-class kid who was ostracized at a tony Chicago Catholic school, McCarthy first burst upon the national pituitary as *Playboy*'s Miss October 1993. (Pretense-free, she says her Playmate photos had "a lot of computerized help.") On MTV, she found a medium in which she is the message—shouting her lines, swinging a plastic mallet, playing manic mama to a raging bullpen of post-teens in heat.

As a junior in film school at the University of Texas, Austin, McConaughey (pronounced Ma-CON-a-hay) was focused on film production until an encounter with a casting director in a local bar led to a small part in 1993's *Dazed and Confused*. Two years later, already cast in a supporting role in *A Time to Kill*, he tested for and got the lead, a Mississippi lawyer defending a black man who kills the white rapists of his daughter. Prerelease screenings started a promotional firestorm touting McConaughey's low-key charisma. Director Schumacher insists there's tinder behind the smoke. "You can't take someone out of the woodwork and make them a star," he told a reporter. "Only God can make a tree."

McCarthy gets pumped on MTV.

He's Grrrreat!

Tiger Woods turns pro, already a millionaire and golf missionary

When Tiger Woods, the 20-year-old new kid on the pro-golf circuit, agreed to play in the Disney World/Oldsmobile Classic in Orlando, the tournament director jumped for joy—into a swimming pool. And why not plunge into the wave of the future? A box-office phenom of Babe Ruthian proportions, Woods had already drawn thousands of new fans in the wake of the greatest professional debut in golf history. And such fans—black teenyboppers, white yuppies, grade-schoolers on a literal field trip. The fairways were alive with the sound of new music: "You go, T! Take care of *bizness*!"

When the Stanford University junior dropped out temporarily to turn pro after sweeping three straight U.S. amateur titles, golf mavens predicted that he might earn enough by year-end to place him in the sport's top 125 and thus win a permanent tour card for '97. Talk about thinking small. Within two months, Woods, having just won at Orlando, was 23rd on the money list, having dominated the game since his entry. One measure of that dominance: In his first seven starts, Woods shot 12 eagles—compared with 14 in 36 tournaments for tour leader Kelly Gibson. On another links ranking, Woods has no golf rival: Nike signed him to a reported five-year, $40-to-$50 million endorsement deal.

The son of a retired Army colonel and his Thai-born wife, Eldrick "Tiger" Woods (nicknamed for a Vietnam buddy of father Earl) was raised to be a Mozart of the fairways. At age 3, he outputted Bob Hope on national TV; by 7, he had begun, under Dad's systematic training, to rule a sport long a bastion of white-only power and privilege (as one Nike ad has stressed). "This is the first black intuitive golfer ever raised in the United States," says Earl. As the fourth-grade fans mimicking his swooshing swing from the sideline suggest, Tiger won't be the last.

Blazing Feet

Savion Glover reinvents tap for the age of rap

At age 4, Savion Glover used to set up his mother's pots and pans and whack them with big spoons until the walls of his Newark, New Jersey, housing project practically shook. Eighteen years later, Glover is bringing down the house nightly at Broadway's Ambassador Theatre. Nowadays he keeps the beat with his feet, thunderously hoofing with a trio of co-dancers in *Bring In 'da Noise, Bring In 'da Funk*, a raucous chronicle of tap dancing in black America—and of black America told through tap dancing. Together with George C. Wolfe, who co-created and directs *Noise*, Glover has imbued an esoteric art with hip-hop rhythms, dazzling moves and a completely new level of percussive intensity. Last June, Glover, 22, won his first Tony for choreography—seven years after earning a Tony nomination at 15 for his role in Broadway's *Black and Blue*. Tap veteran Gregory Hines, who costarred with Glover in the 1992 Broadway musical *Jelly's Last Jam*, attests, "Savion is the best tap dancer that ever lived. He was doing things as a dancer at 10 that I couldn't do until I was 25. He has steps, speed, clarity and an invention that no one else ever had. He's redefined the art form." Glover is aware he has escaped dangerous channels. "If I didn't have the dance to express myself," he says, "I would probably be stealing your car or selling drugs right now. I got friends who do that, but tap saved me." Now, Glover is saving tap.

50TH ANNUAL TONY AWARDS

(Presented June 2, 1996)
Play: *Master Class*, Terrence McNally
Musical: *Rent*
Actor, Play: George Grizzard, *A Delicate Balance*
Actress, Play: Zoe Caldwell, *Master Class*
Actor, Musical: Nathan Lane, *A Funny Thing Happened on the Way to the Forum*
Actress, Musical: Donna Murphy, *The King and I*
Featured Actor, Play: Ruben Santiago-Hudson, *Seven Guitars*
Featured Actress, Play: Audra McDonald, *Master Class*
Featured Actor, Musical: Wilson Jermaine Heredia, *Rent*
Featured Actress, Musical: Ann Duquesnay, *Bring In 'da Noise, Bring In 'da Funk*
Choreography: Savion Glover, *Bring In 'da Noise, Bring In 'da Funk*
Revival, Play: *A Delicate Balance*, Edward Albee
Revival, Musical: *The King and I*

Uno memento: The host fires off a quickie keepsake for her premiere guests, George Clooney and Susan Lucci.

Instant Karma

Sunshine with sass makes Rosie O'Donnell a daytime hit

Her genial, conflict-free talk show, which debuted last June to immediate raves and high ratings, might strike many as a stroke of marketing genius. Rosie O'Donnell spelled relief from the daytime glut of sleaze and weirdness with the conversational equivalent of comfort food—a show modeled after the guest-friendly variety hours of Mike Douglas and Merv Griffin, two of her childhood heroes. But market research couldn't create O'Donnell's mix of under-the-hairdryer yakking and cynical but soft-edged wisecracks, which she lets fly like the Kooshballs she insouciantly flips into the audience. A child of the Long Island suburbs, she is also a deep-fried couch potato—the tube became a surrogate parent in the rough years after cancer took her mother when Rosie was 10. Before she chose daytime TV, O'Donnell had established herself as a stand-up comic and zippy character actress, with film credits including *A League of Their Own* and *Sleepless in Seattle*. But as a single mother, the 34-year-old wanted a job in which she could keep regular hours, avoid travel and spend lots of time with her adopted son, Parker, 2. It seems to be working for Parker, and daytime audiences aren't complaining either.

23RD ANNUAL DAYTIME EMMY AWARDS

(Presented May 22, 1996)
Drama: *General Hospital*
Talk Show: *The Oprah Winfrey Show*
Game Show: *The Price Is Right*
Actress: Erika Slezak, *One Life to Live*
Actor: Charles Keating, *Another World*
Supporting Actress: Anna Holbrook, *Another World*
Supporting Actor: Jerry Ver Dorn, *Guiding Light*
Talk Show Host: Montel Williams, *The Montel Williams Show*
Lifetime Achievement: Phil Donahue

Back with Plenty of Relish

Michael J. Fox puts *Spin City* on the prime-time map, in the process reaffirming his own N.Y. family ties

It was back to the past for Michael J. Fox, 35, who returned to the small screen after a seven-year hiatus to update the Reaganite yupster he played in *Family Ties*. His latest lovable pragmatist is a deputy mayor of the Big Apple, whose *Spin City* mission is to coat his boss in Teflon on issues like gay marriage and needle exchange. Some critics claimed that a flagging film career brought Fox back to TV, but the star has a different spin. He says he wanted to spend more time with wife Tracy Pollan (his *Family Ties* costar) and their three kids, who live in Manhattan, where the series is taped. Either way, with *Spin City* one of the few solid performers of the fall season, Fox is feeling quite at home on the sidewalks of New York.

▲ **DENNIS FRANZ, after copping an Emmy as *N.Y.P.D.*'s Sipowicz, admitted, "I can put on his clothes pretty easily."**

Torre Hallelujah

The humble Yankee skipper shows true heart in the clutch

When the New York Yankees rallied from two crushing World Series defeats at home to beat the Atlanta Braves four straight, their astonish-ing redemption was also manager Joe Torre's. The 37-year veteran had played and managed more than 4,200 games before making it to the Series—the longest drought in base-ball history. Torre, 56, long known by baseball insiders as one of the game's finer human beings, received a flood of public affection.

That was the least of it. On the eve of the Series' final game, Torre's brother Frank, 64, learned that a donor had been found for a lifesaving heart transplant. When Joe arrived in the recovery room two hours after surgery, "they looked at each other and Frank realized who it was," says Dr. Mehmet Oz, the wizard who per-formed the operation. "He lifted up his right hand and Joe kissed it." Talk about victory celebrations. Winning the Series hours later was icing.

Franken Incensed

Al Franken's silly, satirical Rush to judgment is a big fat bestseller

"Fat, fat, fat, fat, fat!" To beat up one of con-servative talk radio's biggest bullies, *Comedy Central* commentator Al Franken got down in the sandbox. His bestselling *Rush Limbaugh Is a Big Fat Idiot* skewers Limbaugh with outra-geous insult and loony lampooning (in one fic-tive scene, Oliver North leads draft evaders Limbaugh, Newt Gingrich, Phil Gramm and George Will on a trek through the Vietnamese jungle). "I wanted to call it 'Rush Limbaugh Is a Big Fat Hypocritical Liar,' " says Franken, 44, "but I felt that was just too confrontational."

He Loved You, Man!

Rob Roy Fitzgerald's career went Budding

As Johnny, the stubbly-face schmo who tries in vain to snag a beer by moaning, "I love you, maaan!" to his dad, his girlfriend and even to a beer deliveryman in three ads for Bud Light, former NFLer Rob Roy Fitzgerald, 40, hit his first real pay dirt in 18 years as an actor. Pleased, but hot to move on (with wife Annie, above), he said, "I don't want 'I love you, man' on my gravestone."

Motley Crew Clicks

The Gardner brothers create a cyberhit called Motley Fool

A fool and his money are soon rolling in it, or at least that's the hope of a brother team who set up an online fount of financial wisdom and stock tips puckishly named Motley Fool after a Shakespearean clown.

Begun as an investment newsletter by David Gardner, 29, Motley Fool floundered until his brother Tom, 27, plugged it onto America Online. Toiling 90-hour weeks in their Alexandria, Virginia, base, they finally rode high in the mid-'90s bull market, generating 6,000 hits a day. They hope to triple their 1995 revenue of $1 million, not including royalties from a bestselling investment guide. David, a onetime writer for PBS's Wall Street guru Louis Rukeyser, says of their feverishly interactive Web site, "In a way, it's the business school of the 21st century."

Giant Killer

Evander Holyfield wins with punch, prayer and a new Mrs.

"I knew what I was going to do," declared Evander Holyfield, "and I was going to be ready for it." He was. Mike Tyson wasn't. The bruising Tyson, who had looked unbeatable in four bouts following his prison release, was dismantled in 11 astonishing rounds by the relentless 7-1 underdog. But Holyfield, 34, who grew up in the Atlanta projects, had help: gospel music during his workouts, fervent prayer and the total support of his new wife, Dr. Janice Itson, an internist whom he had met at a revival meeting in 1994 and married a month before the fight. She shaped up his finances and his family life (he has six kids). "I never could have beaten Tyson without Janice," said the new champ.

New Voice, Old Soul

At 14, country star LeAnn Rimes is already a legend in the making

"I've never sat up at 3 in the morning wondering if a guy is going to come home," admits LeAnn Rimes, who sings about such things in her first major-label single, "Blue"—which sold over 100,000 copies in its first week. But the 14-year-old phenom has "an old soul," as her mother Belinda, 44, has heard many say in response to LeAnn's extraordinary voice, hauntingly reminiscent of Patsy Cline's. And that soul has been gifted from the start with knowledge beyond a child's conscious experience. As Rimes says of tapes recorded before she was out of diapers: "It's kind of cute—I could sing better than I could talk." By age 6, she knew enough to announce, "I'm going to be a big star one day." Though Rimes's first album, *Blue*, soared to the top of the country sales charts by October, the Country Music Awards judges left her empty-handed. But to the judges who matter most—the listening public—she was already Number 1.

30TH ANNUAL COUNTRY MUSIC AWARDS

(Presented October 2, 1996)

Entertainer of the Year: Brooks & Dunn
Male Vocalist: George Strait
Female Vocalist: Patty Loveless
Single: "Check Yes or No," George Strait
Album: *Blue Clear Sky*, by George Strait
Vocal Group: The Mavericks

Vocal Duo: Brooks & Dunn
Music Video: "My Wife Thinks You're Dead," Junior Brown
Horizon Award: Bryan White
Song: "Go Rest High on That Mountain," Vince Gill
Event: Dolly Parton and Vince Gill for "I Will Always Love You"

▼ **BRYAN WHITE, 22, cleaned up on the charts with a clean act. "He's cute," said one fan. "Like a country Michael J. Fox."**

Potent *Little Pill*

Alanis Morissette's jagged but sexy songs prove easy to swallow

She may sound like a woman on the verge of a nervous breakdown, but fans say they find Alanis Morissette's anguished vocals therapeutic. On her Grammy-winning *Jagged Little Pill*, the singer exorcises demons of emotional betrayal in lyrics that range from acerbic to sexually explicit. Morissette became 1996's diva of devastation (her chart-topping song "You Oughta Know" is a hate letter to an ex) and one of several new women rockers—including Joan Osborne, Sheryl Crow and PJ Harvey—to jolt the charts with a wrenching mix of bile and libido. Her provocative image represents a curious about-face for a 22-year-old singer, raised by schoolteacher parents in Ottawa, who started her career at 16 as a squeaky-clean disco queen. "Back then I was a lot more worried about people's perception of me," Morissette said in 1995. "When [old fans] finally heard this more honest part of me, I think they were like, 'Yikes!' " Yikes with a bullet.

38TH ANNUAL GRAMMY AWARDS

(Presented February 28, 1996)

Record of the Year:
"Kiss from a Rose," Seal

Song of the Year:
"Kiss from a Rose," Seal

Album of the Year: *Jagged Little Pill*, Alanis Morissette

New Artist:
Hootie & the Blowfish

Male Pop Vocal:
"Kiss from a Rose," Seal

Female Pop Vocal: "No More I Love Yous," Annie Lennox

Pop Vocal by a Duo or Group: "Let Her Cry,"
Hootie & the Blowfish

Traditional Pop Performance: "Duets II," Frank Sinatra

Rock Song: "You Oughta Know," Glen Ballard, Alanis Morissette

Male Rock Vocal: "Don't You Know How It Feels," Tom Petty

Female Rock Vocal: "You Oughta Know," Alanis Morissette

Rock Vocal by a Duo or Group: "Run-Around," Blues Traveler

R&B Song:
"For Your Love," Stevie Wonder

Male R&B Vocal:
"For Your Love," Stevie Wonder

Female R&B Vocal:
"I Apologize," Anita Baker

R&B Vocal by a Duo or Group: "Creep," TLC

Rap Solo: "Gangsta's Paradise," Coolio

Rap Performance by a Duo or Group: "I'll Be There for You/You're All I Need to Get By," Method Man featuring Mary J. Blige

Hard Rock Performance: "Spin the Black Circle," Pearl Jam

Metal Performance: "Happiness in Slavery," Nine Inch Nails

Alternative Music Album: *MTV Unplugged in New York*, Nirvana

Dynamite, Dignity

Strong, subtle Denzel Washington is PEOPLE's Sexiest Man Alive, 1996

Denzel Washington has probably done fewer steamy scenes than any other Hollywood sex symbol. He is a thinking woman's heartthrob, thanks to his noble bearing and the mostly up-standing, smart characters he has chosen to play—in films including 1996's *Courage Under Fire*, 1992's *Malcolm X* and 1989's *Glory*, for which he won an Oscar as Best Supporting Actor. The son of a strict Pentecostal minister in Mount Vernon, a New York City suburb with a large black population, Washington is devoted to his wife of 13 years, actress Pauletta Pearson, and their four children, as well as a committed member of a West Los Angeles Pentecostal church. "There's a solidness to him as a man," says Sheryl Lee Ralph, who played his wife in 1989's *The Mighty Quinn*. "It's something you can really put your hands on. And I'm sure a lot of women would like to do just that."

Nerd's Revenge

Scott Adams holds a mirror to management with *Dilbert*

Plagued by a heartless boss, confined to a bland cubicle and forced to endure pointless meetings, Dilbert would seem to be one sorry dude. But the tuber-shaped alter ego of cartoonist Scott Adams is a man on the rise. *Dilbert*, the strip, is carried in more than 1,000 newspapers in 32 countries. It's on the Internet, and *The Dilbert Principle*, Adams's book, became a bestseller. Disgruntled employees have made Dilbert's puzzled visage their favorite pinup, a '90s-style symbol of passive resistance. As an engineer at Pacific Bell, Adams himself "had a cubicle-eye perspective" on white-collar woes. Now that he can spend his days drawing at home in California (with girlfriend and two cats for company) Adams, 39, does not lack for material: He receives up to 800 e-mail messages a day from the trenches.

Vats Incredible!

His boutique brews are good for what ales Wicked wonder Pete Slosberg

His face adorns every label, along with an 800 number where he can be reached in his office. "People seem to like the fact that there is a Pete," says Pete Slosberg, 45, founder of Pete's Wicked Ale. Customers and investors like his beer too, which he started brewing in his basement in 1980. Last year, his face launched 345,000 barrels—second most for microbrews.

Simple Solutions

Sarah Ban Breathnach mints a mantra: "All you have is all you need"

In 1993, Sarah Ban Breathnach was an author of two books on Victoriana, a wife and a mother in suburban Washington. But, she says, "I thought I could only be happy if everything was perfect. I wanted to live in a Martha Stewart world." Instead of redecorating, she became "a detective of my own life" and (after 30 publisher's rejections) eventually turned her soul-searching into a book of essays on appreciating life's little pleasures: a tasty meal, a discovery at a tag sale, a talk with a loved one. *Simple Abundance: A Daybook of Comfort and Joy* has sold over a million copies, but was going nowhere until Oprah featured it last spring. Now that's something to appreciate.

No Lightweight

Boxer Christy Martin strikes a blow against gender stereotypes

Last March, when she outpointed Deirdre Gogarty, Christy Martin was bloodied for the first time in her career. That kind of thing is getting harder for Jim Martin, her trainer, to watch. Martin, 5'4", 135 pounds, was the first woman he'd ever coached, and she won both his respect and his heart. The two were married in 1992 and Martin, 28, has since become a gloved sensation, knocking out 25 opponents on the way to a 35-2-2 record. Promoter Don King signed her to a four-year deal, the first woman he has ever taken on, paying her the ultimate boxing compliment: "She can be the Muhammad Ali of female fighters."

Getting Even

At 50, Diane, Bette and Goldie touch a nerve and a funnybone as ex-wives on the warpath

It's the hardiest, most horrendous perennial of women's magazines—the plight of wives jilted for a younger, thinner or richer woman. In *The First Wives Club*, the female feel-good flick of '96, the betrayed exes bond. This cinematic revenge fantasy obviously connected with the collective unconscious of female moviegoers. And not the least of its redemptive pleasures was the renewed marquee magic of its three stars (from left, above, Diane Keaton, Bette Midler and Goldie Hawn), all of them, as it happened, having turned 50. *First Wives* grossed more than $100 million, topping *Thelma and Louise* as one of the most popular women's movies ever. In the film the first wives both embarrass and partially impoverish their previous spouses, humiliate their nubile rivals and then, to add insult to penury, force the men to contribute to a fund for abused women. We're not just talking revenge here, we're talking politically correct reparations.

Real-life exes, of course, rarely rebound so resoundingly. The spouses of celebrities sometimes have it worst of all, forced to regain their footing in a world where their former husbands are idolized. At the supermarket there are tabloids touting photos of the bleeps with new honeys, and, despite the wives' public pain, sympathy may be in short supply, especially if they walk away with a few mil. "My husband was a godlike figure to a lot of strangers," says Lynn Landon, 63, whose 1982 divorce from actor Michael Landon (who wed Cindy Clerico the next year) came after five children and 19 years of marriage. "When he left, he took a lot of me." Landon reclaimed her life by forming a support group called LADIES—Life After Divorce Is Eventually Sane. Olivia Goldsmith, 41, the author of the book upon which *The First Wives Club* is based, recovered after being left by her corporate exec husband in 1984 by the power of her pen. Her literary message was translated into 24 languages and topped many bestseller lists. It's a triumph nearly matching that of the world's most famous dumpee, Ivana Trump, 47, all too publicly tossed aside for Marla Maples. Ivana got $14 million in cash and custody of her three children. As she advises in a spunky cameo in *First Wives*, "Don't get mad. Get everything!"

75

Jackie O on the Auction Block

Legend hunters bid the moon to acquire a piece of Camelot

I T WAS AMERICAN HISTORY—GOING, going, gone—when Jackie-O-philes got their chance to buy a piece of the Kennedy mystique at New York City's famed Sotheby's auction gallery. The catalog—which itself became a collectors' item at $90 per—estimated the worth of the items left by the late First Lady at $5 million, tops. But in four days the 5,000 lots, many of them just knicknacks, were gaveled down for

◄ JACKIE'S PEARLS Jewelry designer Carolee Friedlander paid $83,081 for a faux pearl necklace (like the one JFK Jr. tugged in '62), planning to launch a line of replicas.

an astounding $34.5 million.

Typical of the feeding frenzy was the sale of a humidor Milton Berle had given JFK in 1961 and hoped to reacquire. But the comedian, who had originally paid $800, dropped out at $180,500, long before it was finally sold for $574,500. Joan Rivers successfully bid $13,800 for a 19th-century French painting Sotheby's experts valued at about $1,000. Montel Williams's wife Grace took home a necklace for $17,250. "I didn't care what it cost," said St. Louis socialite Nancy Pillsbury Shirley, who bought an evening bag for $68,500 and was thrilled to find inside a frosted-pink lipstick. Feminist scholar Camille Paglia, who went to observe the mania, said, "One has this sense of the opening of the tomb of a pharaoh and seeing objects that were never intended to be seen by the public."

Some friends of the family, like George Plimpton, chose to stay away, declaring the event unseemly. Said he: "Jackie would not want to be remembered by this sale." Others pointed to the practical side of Jacqueline Kennedy Onassis and of her appreciation of the necessity for raising funds to cover taxes on her $100 to $200 million estate.

"If I had my druthers," said one auction attendee, Manhattan Realtor Kathy Roeder, "I'd want her still here—sitting on her own sofa."

➤ THE ROCK The 40-carat diamond engagement ring from Aristotle Onassis was hammered home for $2.6 million. The apt acquirers (below): Tony O'Reilly, self-made, Irish-born chairman of H.J. Heinz, and his second wife, Chryss Goulandris, a New York-reared Greek shipping heiress.

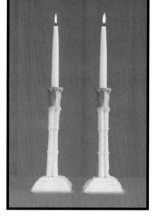

▲ THE CANDLESTICKS These creamware classics were the centerpiece for many a Kennedy dinner (left, in 1959). Valued by Sotheby's at only $250, they commanded $40,250.

STYLE

THE RUNWAYS BRIGHTENED AS BLACK WAS SENT TO
THE CLOSET AND UP POPPED A RIOT OF ANIMAL PRINTS,
SHINY RETRO FABRICS AND FRESH FRUIT-SALAD COLORS

Gucci well suits Jennifer Tilly.

Gotta Getta Gucci

Texan Tom Ford injects new pizzazz into a tired label, and celebs come flocking back

I n the '80s the house of Gucci took a nosedive. The interlocking gold G's, ripped off and emblazoned on everything from T-shirts to handbags, became symbols of tackiness and bad taste. But with Tom Ford, 33, at the helm as creative director since 1994, the ailing fashion house has been reborn. And Gucci (whose stock jumped from $22 to $42 after going public last year) is once again the height of haute. Customers are wait-listed for Ford's techno-stretch pantsuits ($1,645 to $1,750) and silver G white leather pumps ($275). The flagship Milan store can't keep enough of the popular G-belts ($160) in stock.

"Gucci has always been a little flashy, a little Riviera, a little Hollywood—a mix of good taste and bad," says Ford. "Because of the kitsch quality of things now, we came back at the right time. People are saying, 'I'm cool enough to wear this ridiculous G-belt and it's screaming at you, but isn't that great?' " Gucci patrons agree. "When you see Tom's things," says actress Jennifer Tilly, "there's an uncontrollable 'I've got to have it' feeling."

Ford, a native Texan, mastered the art of reinvention long ago. He started with his bedroom, at the age of 5. "I remade my entire room out of cardboard boxes," he remembers. At 12, he had already developed a precursor of his current fashion sense when he pleaded for—and got—a pair of white patent-leather Gucci loafers. "I'd always wanted to be a designer," he says, "but when you grow up in Texas, it's not something you want to admit." In 1986, Ford graduated from Parsons School of Design, and was working with designers Cathy Hardwick and Perry Ellis when Gucci hired him to revamp its ready-to-wear line. A bachelor who is married to his job, he spends barely half a year at his spacious Paris flat. In his off-hours he patrols the club scene from New York to Paris. That, he says, is where he comes up with his best ideas. "I design for the international person who travels between New York, Paris and Hong Kong," he says. "Or at least the person who dreams of such a life."

Elizabeth Hurley dons faux fur.

Kate Winslet takes a sheen.

Hit the Road, Black

A rainbow coalition of stars restores hot color

➤ **IMAN** wore
the ripe stuff.

▼ **MORGAN FAIRCHILD**
has a passion for purple.

▲ **NEON HUSH
PUPPIES** shuffled
into the limelight.

▼ **SANDRA BERNHARD**
shimmered when she
shimmied.

▼ **FAITH FORD**
reflected a celeb
minitrend, the
gold rush.

▼ **PAULA ABDUL**
was electrifying
in thundercloud
blue.

▼ **LAUREN HUTTON**
went luminous in a
stunning two-piecer.

By Their Fruits
Shall Ye Know Them

**Less vampy than black and subtly sexy,
high sheen and bright color made a
splash during the year. Celebs of all
stripes popped up in an a-peeling array
of oranges, lemons and limes, while
others reflected a new urge to glitter in
gold, silver and electric blue.**

80

Animal Magnetism

Fashion was a jungle in 1996—you could almost hear it roar. Animal prints are "very dramatic and fun to wear," says syndicated gossip columnist Liz Smith. Of course, those answering the call of the wild were careful to avoid the howl of PETA: The pelts were correctly faux. With one lively exception. It didn't take Ace Ventura, pet detective, to figure out that actress Tippi Hedren accessorized at an animal-rights promotion in L.A. with her live pet cheetah Subira.

➤ **JAMIE LEE CURTIS** poured herself into a second skin.

➤ **MARY J. BLIGE** was spotted everywhere.

➤ **SUSAN SARANDON** dared frame her fearful symmetry.

➤ **JULIE BROWN** had the cats meowing.

◄ **JERRY HALL** would never be mistaken for a domestic animal.

The Best Dressed And the Not-So

Today's fashion free-for-all yields an embarrassment of riches—and sometimes just a rich embarrassment

◄ **VANESSA WILLIAMS** gleamed like a galaxy in this chain mail gown by Versace.

➤ **Fine tailoring sets off LEEZA GIBBONS's traffic-stopping figure.**

▼ **BRANDY** was brilliant in sequins, cobra coils and sweet-seventeen smile.

➤ **MICHAEL JORDAN** felt no space jam in this relaxed cream suit by personal tailor Alfonso Burdi.

➤ **MOLLY RINGWALD** might bloom like a rose—if she'd only prune her wardrobe.

◄ **Stop! in the name of looks. JOAN OSBORNE's** return to the 1970s made for a bad trip

▼ **Leftover Liberace? STEVEN SEAGAL** swirled up a tapestry travesty.

➤ **TIM ROBBINS** should have quilt while he was ahead.

RST WORST WORST WORST WORST WORST

PEOPLE'S BEST & WORST DRESSED CELEBS OF 1996

BEST	WORST
Vanessa Williams, *33, actress/singer*	Molly Ringwald, *28, actress*
Leeza Gibbons, *39, talk show host*	Helen Hunt, *33, actress*
Sandra Bullock, *32, actress*	Joan Osborne, *34, singer*
Noah Wyle, *25, actor*	Cher, *50, actress*
Brandy, *17, singer*	Steven Seagal, *44, actor*
Jim Carrey, *34, actor*	Cybill Shepherd, *46, actress*
Prince William, *14, future monarch*	Tim Robbins, *37, actor/director*
Gwyneth Paltrow, *23, actress*	Lisa Kudrow, *33, actress*
Michael Jordan, *33, basketball player*	Janeane Garofalo, *31, comedian*
Teri Hatcher, *31, actress*	Dennis Rodman, *35, basketball player*

The Beauties

This year's PEOPLE 50 is Mel mellow and Chili hot

Brooke Shields

Finally at 30 escaping her image of girlish innocence, Brooke Shields stepped into the raunchy Rizzo role in Broadway's *Grease!* and then starred in *Suddenly Susan,* a high-rated update of *The Mary Tyler Moore* show. "She really learned to trust herself," says fiancé Andre Agassi, "and that has sent her beauty over the top."

Keith
Hamilton Cobb

When *All My Children*'s Noah and Julia fled to Jamaica this year, fans of Keith Hamilton Cobb, 34, got their daylight *Baywatch*— a chance to bask in his golden-brown biceps. "Keith has taken off like a rocket," says *AMC* casting director Judy Blye Wilson. Indeed, as his hair grew, so have job offers, and Keith had his last cut in 1988. Costar Sydney Penny says those soft tendrils make love scenes "sort of like *20,000 Leagues Under the Sea.*" That's one ocean *AMC* fans wouldn't mind drowning in.

THE 50 MOST BEAUTIFUL PEOPLE OF 1996

Tori Amos, *32, singer*
Antonio Banderas, *35, actor*
Tyra Banks, *22, model/actress*
Josie Bissett, *25, actress*
Jon Bon Jovi, *34, rock singer*
Brandy, *17, singer/actress*
Pierce Brosnan, *43, actor*
Sandra Bullock, *31, actress*
Patty Cabrera, *27, Christian singer*
Lu Chen, *19, figure skater*
Chili, *25, singer, R&B group TLC*
George Clooney, *35, actor*
Keith Hamilton Cobb, *34, actor*
Johnny Depp, *32, actor*
Fran Drescher, *38, actress*
David Duchovny, *35, actor*
David James Elliott, *35, actor*
Kent Ferguson, *33, diver*
Matthew Fox, *29, actor*
Mel Gibson, *40, actor*
Ed Gordon, *35, TV news reporter*
David Guterson, *40, author*
Laird Hamilton, *32, surfer*
Jack Hanna, *49, zoo director*
Salma Hayek, *27, actress*

Kirsty Hume, *20, model*
Quincy Jones, *63, composer, producer*
Ashley Judd, *28, actress*
Nicole Kidman, *28, actress*
Steve Largent, *41, politician*
Jason and Jeremy London, *23, actors*
Jenny McCarthy, *23, actress*
Demi Moore, *33, actress*
Patrick Muldoon, *27, actor*
Navia Nguyen, *22, model*
Vanessa-Mae Nicholson, *17, violinist*
Chris O'Donnell, *25, actor*
Gail O'Grady, *32, actress*
Michelle Pfeiffer, *38, actress*
Brad Pitt, *32, actor*
Gloria Reuben, *30, actress*
Lela Rochon, *32, actress*
Susan Sarandon, *49, actress*
Brooke Shields, *30, actress*
Mira Sorvino, *28, actress*
Martha Stewart, *54, style czar*
Shannon Sturges, *28, actress*
John Walsh, *50, TV host*
Kate Winslet, *20, actress*

"I'd like to introduce my new bride," John told photographers, as the couple emerged from their Manhattan abode after the honeymoon.

FAMILY MATTERS

Coupling in Camelot

JFK Jr. and his fair lady pull off a wedding coup and come back 1996's most adored newlyweds

IT WAS SIX MONTHS IN THE PLANNING, A brilliant campaign of secrets and subterfuge. John F. Kennedy Jr., aka the World's Most Eligible Bachelor, and his beautiful belle, former Calvin Klein publicist Carolyn Bessette, were married far from the madding crowds of paparazzi. It "required the skill of a James Bond and the whole CIA," said Letitia Baldrige, onetime chief of staff for Kennedy's mother, Jacqueline. "Jackie must be smiling in heaven." The secret wedding took place on Cumberland Island, one mile off the Georgia coast—a tiny wilderness that has little in the way of modern amenities but all the romance needed for a perfect wedding. The only inn is the picturesque white clapboard Greyfield; the only chapel is the First African, a wood-frame structure erected by freed slaves in 1893. The only phone service is cellular. The only access is by ferry and—a rare sight until Thursday, September 19—helicopters. That's when the coterie of illustrious guests began arriving: among them JFK's sister, Caroline Kennedy Schlossberg and her family; Jackie's longtime companion, Maurice Tempelsman; John's uncle Ted Kennedy; and Bessette's mother, Ann Marie, sister Lisa and brother-in-law Michael Roman. Two nights later, the ceremony took place by candlelight and kerosene lamps (the chapel has no electricity), and was accompanied by an a cappella rendition of "Amazing Grace" and "Will the Circle Be Unbroken" by a gospel singer. After a brief Catholic service, guests returned to the Greyfield for the reception.

As Carolyn briefly stood outside in light rain after the ceremony, one of the island's roughly 200 wild horses wandered over and nibbled at her bouquet of lilies of the valley. Partly thanks to signed confidentiality agreements, no one—not caterers, florists, boat captains or inn workers (and certainly not the horses)—had leaked news of the biggest thing ever to hit Cumberland Island, apart from a hurricane. "It was very important for us to be able to conduct this in a private, prayerful and meaningful way with the people we love," said Kennedy. He was, he said, "the happiest man alive.

▲ About 40 guests piled into the First African Baptist Church for the nuptials.

◄ The honeymooners dined al fresco in Istanbul, then cruised the Aegean.

87

Michael Jackson: Living in Spin

It's bye-bye, Lisa Marie; hello, Debbie and Michael Jr.

SHE LIVED IN A MODEST, ONE-bedroom flat in Van Nuys, California, worked as an assistant to a dermatologist, and the only thing glamorous or clamorous about Debbie Rowe, 37, was that she blasted about town on a Harley-Davidson. That changed forever on November 3 when news broke that Rowe was carrying the child of Michael Jackson, 38, and, 11 days later, had wed the King of Pop mid-tour in Australia. The bride, who was six months pregnant, had earlier had a miscarriage, meaning that they had been trying to conceive almost from the moment that Jackson—in his other thunderbolt bulletin of '96—ended his 20-month marriage to Lisa Marie Presley.

The press conjectured that the couple were, in effect, living in spin to reburnish Jackson's image following a child-molestation suit. Though reportedly settled for $15 to $20 mil-lion in '94, the case erupted again after the alleged victim's father filed a new civil suit claiming Jackson had violated the agreement by publically denying there had been any molesta-tion. To shoot down a further nega-tive innuendo, the Jackson camp declared, "Reports speculating that Ms. Rowe was artificially insemi-nated are completely false and irre-sponsible." The singer, meanwhile, described himself as "thrilled. This is my dream come true." The child, a boy, would be named Michael Jr.

The couple met 15 years ago when he was reportedly being treated for vitiligo, a condition that causes loss of skin pigment, in the office of Rowe's boss, Arnold Klein, and she and the doctor had occasion-ally accompanied Jackson on tour. Rowe had been married to a science teacher at her alma mater, Holly-wood High, but they split in 1988 and declared bankruptcy. They were childless, but Rowe has two dogs, a golden retriever and a German shep-herd. She was regarded as a simple, goodhearted woman, most comfort-able in jeans, T-shirts and minimal makeup. She had dated after her divorce, but pals say Jackson wasn't among them. "If anyone has prob-lems, she handles them," says a neighbor, tennis coach Mary Calandro. "She's a great rescuer." When she first told a pal about her pregnancy, Rowe described it as "doing a favor for a good friend."

Friendship blossomed into wedlock when Rowe, who was not with Jackson at the pregnancy announce-ment, flew 14 hours to join him in his two-bedroom hotel suite in Sydney. After a post-concert party, the groom sat down at a piano around 2 a.m. and began thumping out the Wagner wed-ding march. Rowe slipped into some-thing white for the civil ceremony. She spent the next day, her first as Mrs. Michael Jackson, on her own, while the father-to-be, surrounded by his usual entourage of associates and kids, cuddled a koala bear at the Sydney zoo.

"Debbie is not involved in the limelight," said a Jackson aide. "She is very easygoing." By contrast, he noted, "Lisa Marie had a mind of her own." Indeed, Presley, 28, had lived not at Jackson's Neverland ranch but in her own $2.6 million home 90 miles away. In the settlement, each retained their respective fortunes, and Jackson footed the legal bills. No details of Rowe's pre-nup deal were disclosed, but the *London Sun* reported that she got $7.5 million up front and $750,000 a year for life.

▼ In the end, Michael and Lisa Marie (at Euro-Disney in 1994) had only three things in common: celeb childhoods, troubled dads and a penchant for chewing gum.

➤ Rowe told her father that Jackson (with her at a performance of *Sisterella* in Pasadena) "is the most compassion-ate person I have met in my life."

More Smiles Down the Aisle

Clint Eastwood found an anchor, Christie Brinkley an architect, Amy Carter a consultant, Prince a first Mayte

▲ Local TV anchor Dina Ruiz met Clint Eastwood interviewing him in '93. It was Eastwood, 65, who popped the question in '96. Ruiz, 30, said yes.

▲ Clothing designer Brad Becker-man, 30, was so jazzed by his bride, pop singer Paula Abdul, 33, that he gave her an unscripted smooch in mid-ceremony. "Don't use it up *now*!" cried the rabbi.

➤ "Amy said she didn't belong to anyone," former President Jimmy Carter proudly noted after daughter Amy, 28, marched solo down the aisle to wed computer consultant Jim Wentzel, 28.

◄ A supermodel goes off with her rocker: Wonderbra showcase Eva Herzigova, 23, joined hands with Bon Jovi drummer Tico Torres, 42. Bandmates Jon Bon Jovi and Richie Sambora were ushers.

▼ On the set of his syndicated TV series *Renegade*, actor Lorenzo Lamas, 38, found one bikini-clad extra special. So he made his fourth trip down the aisle, uniting with model Shauna Sand, 24.

▲ On Valentine's Day, marrying dancer Mayte Garcia, he became, at 37, the Artist Formerly Known as a Bachelor.

➤ Architect Peter Cook, 37, got a package deal: Christie Brinkley, 42, and two stepkids.

▼ It was Miller time for 39-year-old Daniel Day-Lewis—with a new film of Arthur Miller's *The Crucible* and a new bride, the playwright's daughter Rebecca, 34. The couple plan to divide their time between New York City and County Wickow, Ireland.

▲ Dennis Hopper, 59, and actress Victoria Duffy, 28, who met two years ago, toasted each other after marrying at Boston's Old South Church. Then it was on to Italy. Hopper has three children by four previous wives.

➤ Model, actress and disco diva Grace Jones, 43, wore a white lace bustier when she wed her Turkish bodyguard, Atila Altaunbay, 21, in Rio de Janeiro. The minister, according to later reports, was defrocked some years before.

◄ Nadia Comaneci, 34, and her longtime American beau Bart Connor, 38, both Olympic gold-medal gymnasts, exchanged vows in her native Romania in April, the first marriage for both. They run a gymnastics school in their adopted hometown of Norman, Oklahoma.

Love Connection

Cybill got a ring, Whoopi got cuddly with a costar, Sharon Stone gathered no moss

Sharon Stone, 38, changed beaus faster than jewelry: first, L.A. restaurateur Brad Johnson, 39 (lower left); next, musician Dweezil Zappa, 26 (left); Guess? exec Michel Benasera (below); by November, it was Columbia production boss Barry Josephson, 40.

▲ Cybill Shepherd, 45, betrothed herself to musician Robert Martin, 46.

◄ Whoopi Goldberg, 47, and fellow-actor Frank Langella, 56, ended their respective marriages and hooked up while making the Disney comedy *Eddie*. Whoopi reportedly fought to have Langella's name placed alongside hers in the credits, though his role was smaller.

➤ *Cable Guy* Jim Carrey, 34, and his longtime girlfriend, actress Lauren Holly, 32, of *Picket Fences*, each gave marriage a second go, tying the knot in Malibu.

A Labor-Intensive Year

Madonna reinvents herself, this time as a mom

AFTER PLAYING PUNKISH "BOY Toy" in the early '80s and "Material Girl" in mid-decade, Madonna switched to outrage in the early '90s. She tossed her panties to David Letterman, painted the town with women on her arm and published an explicit picture book called *Sex.* But album sales sagged and public attention lagged. So last year, at a restless 38 and counting, she took the national pulse once more and finally got her chakras correctly lined up. Meet the all-improved '96 model Madonna: mother, movie star, matron-next-door.

She had identified with Eva Perón, the charismatic wife of the Argentine dictator, whose life she brought to the screen. "People were angry with Evita," she wrote in a diary for *Vanity Fair,* "for the same reason they are angry with me today. We are women with success and power." Even before the film's Christmas premiere, her star amperage seemed re-juiced. In November, "You Must Love Me," from the *Evita* soundtrack, debuted at No. 22, and designers got busy running up Evita-esque frocks. The surge had started a few weeks earlier when she delivered what she calls "the greatest miracle of my life:" a daughter named Lourdes Maria Ciccone Leon.

It was not an easy birth. Her labor began at 3:30 a.m. on October 14 and continued for 12 hours until doctors advised giving up her planned natural birth for sedation and a C-section. "Goodbye, everyone," said Madonna, as they wheeled her away. "I'm going to get my nose job now." At 4:01 p.m.,

Lourdes came into the world at 6 lbs., 9 ozs. (The obstetrician was Paul Fleiss, dad of Hollywood madam Heidi Fleiss.) At Madonna's side in the delivery room was the sire, Carlos Leon, 30, her former personal trainer and quasi-boyfriend. Though she had told Forrest Sawyer on *Prime Time Live* in December 1995 that she would take a personal ad to find Mr. Right for "the fatherhood gig," she had, in fact, met Leon 15 months before, while running in Manhattan's Central Park. He was sweet, shy, and totally toned. While Leon remains in the background, and Madonna wouldn't reveal how involved he would be in raising Lourdes, her publicist, Liz Rosenberg, said, "He is definitely in the picture" (and in a small recurring role on CBS's *Nash Bridges*).

What won't be in any pictures, Madonna hoped, is Lourdes. "I won't be doing anything in public with my daughter until she's much older," she declared. Earlier in the year, Madonna was relieved to see a stalker who had threatened her life receive a 10-year sentence. And she had left her startling pink mansion in the Hollywood Hills for a more baby-friendly, one-story in the lower profile L.A. neighborhood of Los Feliz. A few weeks before Lourdes arrived in her new floral-decorated nursery, Madonna had dinner for Leon and some of her family, and did what a relative hadn't seen her do in years: the dishes. She also steeped herself in the literature ("Which baby book *haven't* I read?") and noted that "the whole world wants to give me advice." One of the few people she might listen to, Rosie O'Donnell, warned her of what lay ahead. "I told her," said O'Donnell, by then a 17-month veteran of motherhood, "it's going to change her in the best possible way."

◄ She did a daily hour of aerobics and never suffered morning sickness, but called giving birth "the hardest thing I've ever done—also the greatest."

▼ Leon reportedly got ticked and left during the *Evita* soundtrack recording in London, but was with Madonna on location in Argentina and at this Versace show in Paris.

➤ Tommy, can you hear me? Parenthood has mellowed Pamela (with Brandon). Can her hubby adjust?

Wake-Up Call

New mom Pamela Lee files for divorce —just until Tommy gets the message

Since he's as tattooed as an old-fashioned sailor, maybe she thought she'd fire a warning shot across his bow. With just a shape-up-or-ship-out message, *Baywatch* star Pamela Anderson Lee, 29, apparently made her point. Two weeks after filing for divorce from Mötley Crüe drummer Tommy Lee, 34, on November 19, citing "irreconcilable differences," she took him back, saying through her publicist that she was going to support him "in his battle with alcohol abuse."

There had been strains, of course, as in any marriage. A home video, documenting the couple's lovemaking while speeding in a car and in a boat, was stolen, according to a suit the couple filed to prevent publication in *Penthouse.* She reportedly claimed he forced her to make the tape. And by some accounts, Lee—who was arrested for abuse (no charges were filed) when he lived with model Bobbi Brown in 1994—was driven to jealous fury by any mention of his wife's past lovers.

The birth of Brandon last June may have shed a cold light on such shenanigans. While Pamela was mellowing into a doting mom, one who brings her son to the *Baywatch* set, Tommy was still marching to his own drumbeat. "The pace will pick up [after the baby's birth]," he told *USA Today* in May. "When I get older, that's when it'll be time to shut it down. For now, it's 'Let's go.' " Pamela may have wanted to put a stop to that for Brandon's sake. But this is a woman who doesn't make a point just once. Shortly after she and Tommy wed on a beach in Cancún, Mexico, in 1995, they exchanged vows again, in her L.A. backyard, in silver space suits. Then last September she surprised him at a recording session and whisked him back to Cancún for a third wedding—in a bar, with a cabbage for a bouquet. Nuptials are running ahead of nevermores—so far.

New Arrivals

The stars become producers of their own family hits

◄ **Five months married, Antonio Banderas, 36, and Melanie Griffith, 39, welcomed 5-lb., 7-oz. daughter Stella del Carmen into the world.**

▲ **"I've been blessed with two miracles in nine weeks," said Sly Stallone, 50, after the girl born to fiancée Jennifer Flavin, 28, had successful heart surgery.**

◄ **She's micro, she's soft, she's Jennifer Katharine, first child of software magnate Bill Gates, 40, and Melinda French Gates, 31.**

▲ ***Home Improvement*'s Debbe Dunning, 30, and Olympic volley-baller Steve Timmons, 38, brought home a daughter in December.**

◄ Hard labor turned out happily for Natasha Richardson, 33, wife of Liam Neeson, 44, who gave birth to their second child, Daniel Jack.

▼ Woody Harrelson, 35, and his former personal assistant Laura Louie, 30, were cheered by the arrival of an 8-lb. daughter, Zoe, in Costa Rica. The couple also has a 3-year-old daughter, Deni.

▼ Richard Thomas, 45, once *The Waltons'* John-Boy, cut the umbilical cord when second wife Georgiana, 36, bore a boy, Montana, at their L.A. home.

▲ Tennis broadcaster and art dealer John McEnroe, 36, watched the U.S. Open with fourth child, Anna, his daughter with singer Patty Smyth, 37, who also has a girl, 9.

▲ Ella Rose (7 lbs., 13 ozs.) made Keith Richards, 52 (with wife Patty Hansen), the second Stone to become a grandpa, after Mick.

➤ Anthony, the mighty Quinn, 81, and companion Kathy Benvin, 34, produced Ryan Nicholas, who joins sister Antonia, 2.

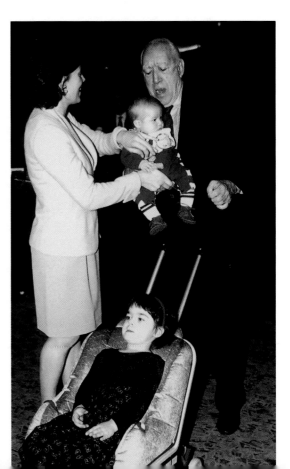

Celebs Asunder

Van Damme kicked the hubby habit, Fran and her man surprisingly split, Liz and Larry are officially bulldozed

➤ Jean-Claude Van Damme, 35, was booted by Darcy LaPier, 30.

▲ Martin Lawrence, 31, and wife Patricia Southall, 25, had it to the brim.

➤ Cover gal Niki Taylor, 21, and football hunk Matt Martinez, 25, filed for divorce.

Vanessa Williams, 33, and former manager-husband Ramon Hervey, 33, separated.

◀ Calvin, 53, and Kelly Klein, 39, married nearly 10 years, announced a split in August, saying they intend to remain "the closest of friends."

Former N.Y.C. high school sweethearts Fran Drescher and Peter Marc Jacobson, both 39, parted after 18 years of marriage, although neither uttered the "D" word. Jacobson is expected to continue in his role as executive producer of her hit sitcom *The Nanny.*

▲ Elizabeth Taylor, 64, and her seventh spouse, Larry Fortensky, 44, divorced in November after 52 months, one of Taylor's longer runs in matrimony. Given a $3,000-a-month living allowance by Taylor last August, the ex-construction worker, who claims he cannot live in the style he grew used to with Liz, is battling for more of her millions. Stay tuned.

◄ Charlie Sheen, 30, and his wife, model Donna Peele, 25, split after 5 months.

► Teri Garr, 46, and contractor husband John O'Neil, 44, decided to dissolve it.

◄ Halle Berry, 29, and Atlanta Braves slugger David Justice, 30, whiffed after three years.

▼ Luciano Pavarotti's trysts with his secretary, 27, finitoed his 35-year marriage.

101

Wills the Conqueror

At 14, the Prince likes cool clothes and hot cars but keeps the ladies in waiting

WITHIN THE LAST YEAR, HIS sense of destiny has come upon him much more strongly," says a palace insider of Prince William, 14. "It's tough, but he's coping with it." Monarchs-in-waiting have always borne a weighty burden, but William Arthur Philip Louis Windsor is the first to hit puberty in the era of predatory paparazzi, tell-all tabloids and breathless teenzines. The British teen bible *Smash Hits* proclaimed young Wills well endowed with snogability—i.e., the ability to make teen girls hyperventilate. It was not an idle call: The publication cashed in big time at the newsstands with an issue featuring a pullout of a blue-blazered William and a follow-up that contained an I LOVE WILLY sticker. Rival teenybop publications jumped aboard, according the prince the gaga adulation usually reserved for movie, telly and rock stars.

While less reserved boys might revel in the notoriety, William has inherited his father's generally deco-

rous sensibility. "He cringes at things like the *Smash Hits* poster," says *Daily Mail* correspondent Richard Kay, a confidant of Princess Diana's. "He doesn't enjoy public life." Diffidence aside, he is being counseled by Prince Charles's staff on such matters as scheduling photo ops—and, more uncomfortably, by both parents in dealing with the divorce. At Eton, where he is a solid if not stellar scholar, he receives no

◄ **William (left) joins classmates for a stroll at Eton where he has been accepted as one of the boys.**

special treatment, but school officials have threatened to expel anyone who prattles about him to the press. Though formal training for his role as king will not start until he is 18, a sense of royal destiny is being instilled in him by his grandmother the Queen. "She might show him a letter written by Henry VIII or from Queen Victoria to Disraeli," says author Brian Hoey, "to give him a sense of what his role will be."

For now, William seems determined to carve out an ordinary boy's life for himself—no small accomplishment in his fishbowl existence. He is partial to video games, mountain bikes, driving Dad's Range Rover and hunting—he shot his first stag and was daubed with the blood as a rite of passage. Already approaching his mum's height of 5'10", he dresses in only the naffest gear: designer sneakers, Benetton threads and baseball caps. In his locker at Eton he keeps a pinup of *Baywatch* babe Pamela Anderson Lee, and he happily met Cindy Crawford, whom Mum invited to tea for him.

Attending his first teen dance at London's Hammersmith Palais, he took to the floor only with acquain-

▲ His natural athleticism has helped him fit in. He sculls (here on the Thames), plays soccer and water polo.

tances, waving his arms in the air to the music. Friends fended off more aggressive partners who asked, "Would you like to snog with me?" After the soiree, reports Richard Kay, "William told his mother, 'Lots of girls tried to kiss me, but I didn't do anything because the cameras are everywhere.' " Such renunciations and innate decorum may prove to be the salvation for the currently snogged-up House of Windsor.

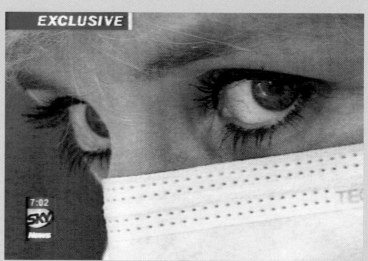

◄ Last March, soon after it was announced that Di had agreed to a divorce, the Princess retreated to the North London home of her long-time friend and therapist Susie Orbach, 49, author of *Fat Is a Feminist Issue.*

▲ Di stirred dissent by observing cardiac surgery on a 7-year-old boy in England last April. Fine, said critics, but did TV cameras have to be present?

▲ The marriage seemed endless, but it took only a few seconds, on July 11, for Di and Prince Charles to sign the divorce papers that formally ended it.

◄ At the Chicago fund-raiser, millionaire toolmaker Michael Wilkie broke protocol by asking Di to dance without prior arrangement. Unruffled, she accepted.

Di-vorced but Not Derailed

Charity cheers the Princess

She dazzled, she danced and she delighted. It was clear from the visit of the former Royal Highness to Washington last September—and from a swing through Chicago in June—that America still loves Di and vice versa. No wonder. The home front has not been a happy place for her. In July, at London's Somerset House—before the judge who presided over the divorces of Princess Anne, Prince Andrew and Camilla Parker Bowles—Diana and Prince Charles began the process. Di's lawyer, Anthony Julius, didn't quite deliver the "divorce deal of the century" he boasted of to the British tabs, but he got his client $23 million up front, plus a $600,000 yearly allowance for expenses related to her office, a nine-room apartment in Kensington Palace and her jewels (estimated value, $30 mil).

What she lost was symbolic but significant: the right to call herself Her Royal Highness (she is to be known as Diana, Princess of Wales) and inclusion in the Church of England's daily Prayer for the Royal Family. Strict rules of royal etiquette would now require her to curtsy to lesser royals like Fergie's daughters. But experts don't think that will actually happen. One palace insider said Di was finally just relieved to end the misery and wanted "to concentrate on the issues she really cared about." Those include breast cancer, children's hospitals and AIDS charities. Di's royal status may be diminished, but her star power here is undimmed. In Washington she hosted a charity sale for breast cancer research. Proceeds: more than $1 million.

▲ Unflappable Fergie, 37, took daughters Eugenie, 6 (second from left), and Beatrice, 8 (not pictured), to an English park, seemingly unconcerned about her $4.6-million debt (offset somewhat by a $3-million divorce settlement from Prince Andrew). Her bestselling '96 autobiography, *My Story*, promised to further boost her bottom line.

More than a Bad Hair Day

Monaco endures marital and medical minidramas

One was a victim of heartless cruelty, the other went mysteriously hairless. And every tabloid in the world was speculating on what was up with the princesses of Monaco in 1996.

In September, Stephanie, 31, filed for divorce from her bodyguard-turned-husband, Daniel Ducruet, also 31, two weeks after European magazines ran pictures of him frolicking with a former Miss Bare Breasts of Belgium. Around the same time, glamorous 39-year-old Princess Caroline was photographed leaving her home in Saint-Rémy-de-Provence at the wheel of her car, minus the Royal mane (below). "It's a skin problem," Prince Albert, 38, told PEOPLE. "Other than that, she's fine." While the palace would not issue any kind of formal explanation about the mysterious condition, the bald pate was obviously not an intentional attempt to emulate Sinéad O'Connor.

WE BID ADIEU TO TREASURES LIKE GENE KELLY AND
ELLA FITZGERALD, AND TO TRAGIC FIGURES LOST TOO
SOON, LIKE MARGAUX HEMINGWAY AND MIKE BOORDA

TRIBUTE

George Burns

From vaudeville to divine comedy, he played it straight to deliver a century of love and laughter

George Burns had a joke about his longevity. "I'm going to stay in show business until I'm the only one left"—and he very nearly made good on his promise. Teddy Roosevelt was President when 7-year-old Nathan Birnbaum first took the stage as a singer in the Peewee Quartet. By the time he died, the fourth-grade dropout from the teeming streets of Manhattan's Lower East Side was 100 years old and, if not the last comic, then one of the last to have started in vaudeville. He found his sweet spot in radio, TV, nightclubs, books and movies, but he didn't hit his career peak until he was in his 80s, when he played the Supreme Being in three hit *Oh God* movies. "Why shouldn't I play God?" he quipped. "Anything I do at my age is a miracle."

For Burns, self-deprecation was a way of life. "I had a very special talent," he'd say. "Gracie Allen." But during his years with Gracie, he was

Playing themselves, Burns and Allen starred in some 20 films, including *College Swing* in 1938.

arguably the greatest straight man ever, a perfectly imperturbable foil for his wife's strenuous exercises in making sense. It was Burns who wrote much of the scatterbrained material that Allen delivered with such cockeyed charm. Mel Brooks saw through the straight-man act, declaring Burns, "the most focused and economical comedian who ever lived."

Maybe both men were right. When Burns met Gracie in 1922, she was a secretarial student and a part-time performer and he'd been a struggling showman for almost 20 years. Smitten, he persuaded the 17-year-old to feed him set-up lines.

After gauging the audience reaction at their first few stage appearances, Burns realized he had it backward. Gracie was getting all the laughs. He rewrote the act—and shaped her into "the dizziest dame in the world," as he put it, but one who acted "as if she were totally sane, as if her answers actually made sense."

In effect, Burns had two careers. His first ended when Gracie died of a heart attack in 1964. He was shattered. But, gradually, he came to terms with Gracie's death, comforting himself by sleeping in her bed (they had separates) and visiting her grave monthly to "tell her everything that's going on. I don't know if she hears me, but I do know that every time I talk to her, I feel better." He might have settled into a comfortable retirement, but instead he moved on to become something unique—a wry advance man in the world of very old age, scouting the fringes of life and sending back funny dispatches to the rest of us. At 79, he triumphed as a retired vaudevillian in *The Sunshine Boys*, his first film since 1938. The performance won Burns an Oscar for Best Supporting Actor—and launched him on his second career.

In his later years, Burns could be seen at lunch most days at the Hillcrest Country Club in Beverly Hills. He would take two martinis, a bowl of soup and a bite of everything each person at his table was having. Then he would adjourn with friends, such as billionaire oilman Marvin Davis, to play bridge. He had no doubt that in the next life he would rejoin Gracie. When she died, Burns had arranged for Episcopal rites although she was Roman Catholic. His explanation was pure Gracie: "I want to be buried with Gracie, and since I'm Jewish, I can't be buried in Catholic-consecrated ground. I hope the Episcopal rites were the right compromise." How could heaven resist?

Ron Brown

A charismatic
Washington power
broker dies on a
mission of peace

To war-ravaged Bosnia, Commerce Secretary Ron Brown sought to apply the balm of American investment. His mission as he saw it was "to turn commerce into the infrastructure of democracy"—and to expand U.S. markets in the process. When the Air Force jet bearing Brown, 24 U.S. officials and business leaders, and six crewmen smacked into a Croatian mountain, leaving no survivors, Brown, 54, died doing what he did best—fusing deal-making and peacemaking. The crash terminated his stunning transformation of a once lightly regarded Cabinet post into a power center—and of Brown, a former Jesse Jackson liberal, into the darling of U.S. business and the Administration's most influential African-American.

Brown's success as a power broker probably would not have surprised anyone who knew him growing up in New York City. His father managed Harlem's storied Hotel Theresa, a magnet for many black celebrities playing the nearby Apollo Theater. Young Ron built up a brisk trade in autographs, perhaps developing the skills that would make him one of Washington's most powerful lobbyists in the 1980s—and propel him to the chairmanship of the Democratic National Committee in 1989. His aptitude for wheeling and dealing also caused him trouble; at the time of his death, he was under investigation for alleged influence peddling.

Brown's friends and colleagues could barely conceive that someone so dynamic could simply be gone. "He had an incurable optimism about the possibilities of life," says former law partner Timothy May. "He made people believe that the things they imagined could be done."

Margaux
Hemingway

Papa's granddaughter
consumed herself in
fame and the fast life

"Help me," said the pager of chiropractor Caren Elin, a longtime friend of model and actress Margaux Hemingway. In hindsight, the message, about a minor problem, was more portentous than it seemed. In an eerie phone call around the same time, Hemingway told Elin she was planning a long trip and asked her friend what she thought about near-death experiences. Just a few weeks later the granddaughter of literary luminary Ernest Hemingway, who had killed himself 35 years earlier, was found dead at 41 from what the Los Angeles County coroner said was a deliberate overdose of the phenobarbital she used for her epileptic seizures.

In 1975, Hemingway won a million-dollar contract for Fabergé's Babe perfume. But a sybaritic life in the 1980s with the Studio 54 set cost her the job and left her struggling with bulimia, depression and a serious drinking problem. "In my grandfather's time it was a virtue to drink a lot and never show it," Hemingway once said. "And, like him, I wanted to live my life to the fullest, with gusto. I always thought alcohol would give me the strength and courage to do whatever I do."

Both her marriages, first to marketing entrepreneur Errol Wetson and later to Venezuelan film director Bernard Foucher, disintegrated within a few years. But mourning friends and relatives found the coroner's ruling hard to accept because Hemingway had recently moved into a sunny new apartment she loved in Santa Monica, had begun avidly practicing yoga and meditation and was reviving her career with roles in TV movies. "This was the best I'd seen her in years," said Steve Crisman, husband of Hemingway's younger and more successful actress sister Mariel. "She had gotten herself back together."

Audrey Meadows

Prime-time's proto-feminist held her own opposite
the Great One in 39 episodes that will live forever

Her Alice Kramden was TV's first no-
nonsense heroine—the mother of all
Roseannes, the un-Lucy. In the course
of just 39 episodes, she made Alice in-
delible: long-suffering but nobody's

fool, defiantly staring down her roaring
water buffalo of a husband, Jackie Gleason's Ralph, and thudding him back to
reality with verbal jujitsu. "This is
probably the biggest thing I've ever got

into!" Ralph once enthused about one
of his grandiose schemes. Retorted
Alice: "The biggest thing you ever got
into is your pants." Yet when he tum-
bled, Alice was always there to put
Humpty-Dumpty together again.

After *The Honeymooners*, Meadows
worked sporadically, preferring to
devote herself to her second husband,
Continental Airlines CEO Robert Six
(her first marriage, to a Washington
Realtor, lasted just two years). The

Greer Garson

As the memorable Mrs. of World War II-era film, she made stalwart, selfless devotion sexy

Often cast as a wholesomely sexy homemaker, Greer Garson radiated self-less devotion in *Goodbye, Mr. Chips* (1939) and won her only Oscar (she was nominated seven times) as the brave British housewife who endured German air raids in 1942's *Mrs. Miniver*. Garson's father, an Irish business-man, died when she was an infant and, soon after, she moved to London with her mother. A gangly, sickly child, she matured into a striking redhead who, with her poise and elegant diction, was discovered on the London stage by Louis B. Mayer. The actress, who died of heart failure at 92, played so many matrimonial roles at Mayer's MGM that she used to say that, in her case, the initials stood for "Metro's Glorified Mrs." "There were jokes like the one that I was the human Lassie," the thrice-married actress once said. "But there are worse images."

couple were inseparable from their 1961 wedding until Six's death in 1986, trav-eling the world and enjoying homes in Denver, New York City and Beverly Hills.

Audrey's big sister and closest friend, actress Jayne Meadows, 74, held her in her arms before she succumbed to lung cancer at 69. "I spoke in her ear," Jayne said afterward. "I used the names we used to call each other as kids in New York City." To the rest of us, Audrey remains forever Alice.

Gene Kelly

An exuberant everyman, he reinvented dance on screen

Simple things like roller skates and rain puddles brought out the best in Gene Kelly, who died in his sleep at his Beverly Hills home at 83, debilitated by a series of strokes. As actor, dancer, choreographer and director, he imparted a sense of grace to the ordinary stuff of life: the raucous joy of a sailor on shore leave in *Anchors Aweigh;* trash-can lids that could become tap shoes in *It's Always Fair Weather;* the ridiculous bliss of a guy in love in *Singin' in the Rain.*

"His appeal was his simplicity. He wasn't the elite, he didn't play a gentleman," says Leslie Caron, 64, who starred with Kelly in his Oscar-winning *An American in Paris.* "Gene was the everyday man." A self-described "working-class stiff" from Pittsburgh, he dropped out of college temporarily in 1930 to help support his family. He pumped gas and dug ditches—life experiences that shaped his art. "As a Depression-era kid who went to school in some very bad times," he told *The New York Times,* "I didn't want to move or dance like a rich man."

He did move and dance like no one before or after him, though. Underpinning his ordinary-Joe persona was music and dance training, the athleticism of a Michael Jordan and an uninhibited joy of movement that was all his own. Fred Astaire's nimble footwork and tuxedo-clad elegance had set a standard for male dancers, but Kelly bounded through numbers in huge, athletic strides, performing in polo shirts, khakis and dazzling white socks that drew the eye to his fancy footwork.

First as a dancer and then as a choreographer, Kelly reinvented dance on screen. "I felt the dancer in films had never had the opportunity to probe emotional and acting problems adequately," Kelly once said. "So I tried to do things uniquely cinematic that you couldn't do on a stage. Call it 'cine-

dancing' or whatever, but I tried to invent the dance to fit the camera and its movements." In the process, he pioneered such technical innovations as dancing with his mirror image (in 1944's *Cover Girl)* and cavorting with the animated cartoon mouse Jerry in *Anchors Aweigh.*

After financing his schooling by giving 50-cents-an-hour dance lessons, he finally graduated from the University of Pittsburgh in 1933 and founded the soon-flourishing Gene Kelly Studios of the Dance. Five years later, he set out for New York City, unworried about getting a job, because he thought, "the other dancers weren't that good." By 1940 he was starring in the musical *Pal Joey;* in 1942 he made his screen debut in *For Me and My Gal,* opposite Judy Garland. By 1949 he had won control of his own projects, choreographing as well as dancing in *Take Me Out to the Ball Game* and the exhilarating *On the*

Town—the first musical to be shot on location (in which he costarred with Frank Sinatra, left). *An American in Paris* carried off seven Oscars in 1952, including Best Picture and a special award for Kelly, inspired by a memorable 17-minute ballet dramatizing the hero's encounter with the City of Light.

In 1960, Kelly married a second time, to his assistant choreographer and former dance student Jeanne Coyne. When she died of leukemia in 1973, Kelly put his career on hold to devote himself to their children, Timothy, now 33 and a film director, and Bridget, 31, a costume designer. In 1990, Kelly married writer Patricia Ward, 37, who was helping him with a never-completed autobiography.

Speaking of his masterpiece, 1952's *Singin' in the Rain,* Kelly summed up his credo: "The picture was done with joy, and it brings joy. That's what I always tried to do."

McLean Stevenson

*M*A*S*H*'s* Colonel Blake was in many ways the real McLean

McLean Stevenson, who played *M*A*S*H*'s* sweet if slightly addled Col. Henry Blake, "had this wonderful midwestern innocence," says series executive producer Gene Reynolds. "He *was* Henry Blake." Though Stevenson left in 1975 after only three seasons (and starred in several subsequent failed sitcoms), he remained identified with Blake, whom he had patterned after his dad, a cardiologist. When Stevenson, 66, died of a heart attack, his friends mourned that he was again gone too soon.

Ray Combs

The *Feud* host lost his job—and his world

Ray Combs seemed the ideal host for *The New Family Feud*—cheerful and perfectly in tune with the pinball rhythms of game shows. But after he was replaced as host in 1994, a car crash left him with permanent spinal pain, and a series of business failures sent him into a tailspin that ended in the collapse of his 18-year marriage, which had produced six children. In June, Combs, 40, was admitted to a psychiatric ward after bashing his head bloody against a wall at home. The next day, he

hanged himself with sheets in the closet of his room.

Though he spent two years as a Mormon missionary, Combs always wanted to be a comic, and after a breakthrough standup gig on *The*

Tonight Show, he was offered *Feud*. But ratings never took off, and in 1994 he was let go. "Losing *Feud* was a huge blow," says its director, Marc Breslow, "because it became his world."

Timothy Leary

Hooked on alternative realities, the guru of
LSD takes his last—and most cosmic—trip

In 1960, Timothy Leary ate a mushroom
in Mexico, and life was never the same.
He liked the effect of the hallucino-
genic fungus and before long became
an evangelist of the psychedelic-en-
hanced life. Fired from the psychology
faculty of Harvard, he was declared by
Richard Nixon "the most dangerous
man in America."

Leary dropped acid with Jack Ker-
ouac, hung out with John and Yoko and
the Chicago Seven, married five times

and did jail time for marijuana convic-
tions. His motto was, "Turn on, tune in
and drop out." In later life he got
hooked on the alternative realities of
the Internet, which he called "the LSD
of the future." A self-promoter to the
end, Leary turned his own death, of
prostate cancer at 75, into a cyberhap-
pening, chronicling his illness and daily
drug intake on a personal Web site.
Then, for a finale, he hired a Houston
firm to launch his ashes into orbit.

John Chancellor

The contemplative commentator and anchor preferred sailing the seas of breaking news to riding a desk

From his days as a teenage copyboy on the *Chicago Daily News*, John Chancellor's first love was always reporting. The only child of Chicago hotel owner Estil and his wife, Mollie, he was known for grace under fire—literally, while covering a civil war in Lebanon in 1958, and figuratively, a year earlier during the school-integration crisis in Little Rock, Arkansas, where the young NBC-TV reporter was jeered on-camera by an angry mob. Though he became a *Today* star in the '60s, the *NBC Nightly News* anchor in the '70s and a thoughtful commentator in the '80s, Chancellor was happiest sprung from the desk. "Those of us who came out of newspapers tried to set standards that attempted to divorce us from television's entertainment aspects," says former CBS news anchor Walter Cronkite. "John was a principal fighter in that battle, leading the charge and keeping the pressure on NBC in that regard."

Diagnosed with stomach cancer after his 1993 retirement, Chancellor died two days before his 69th birthday. He faced the end with characteristic courage, helped by Barbara, his wife of 38 years. "I thought I would live a happy life after NBC, and then fate ambushed me," he mused. "But I'm alert now to some of the very simple pleasures of life: a good meal, a satisfying book, a soft breeze. And Barbara and I have never been closer."

Tommy Rettig

Lassie's first master struggled to master life after a starring start

When he died of arteriosclerosis at 54, Tommy Rettig still received fan mail from those who remembered him as the little boy who had thrown big hugs around the neck of TV's most intrepid collie. Rettig's career began at 5, when an acting coach in the family's apartment building in Queens, New York, spotted the towhead with the lovable grin. He landed his defining role at 12, in 1954, but after four years of *Lassie*, Rettig had trouble getting work, and in the '70s was busted for possession of marijuana. Following a divorce (he took pride in being the father of two sons) he pulled himself together and in his last years ran a successful home-based business, designing computer software.

Greg Morris

The *Mission Impossible* team suffers its first loss

Long before the *Friends* cast was hailed for being best buddies, *Mission Impossible* brewed up some lasting chemistry along with the intricate, improbable plots that drove it from 1966-73. "We genuinely liked each other," Greg Morris, who played electronics ace Barney Collier (center), once explained. "That's what made the show a hit."

The son of a trumpet player who left home when his son was 3, Morris was married to his wife Lee for 37 years, and two of his three children followed him into acting. His relationships with the *MI* cast were equally adhesive. More than two decades after the show ended the *MI* friends were still close, and helped see their pal Morris through two bouts of cancer and a near-fatal 1981 car crash. When Morris died of unspecified natural causes at 62, his former costars were stricken. "Losing Greg hurts like a body blow," said Barbara Bain. Says *Mission* costar Peter Lupus: "It's hard to believe one of us is gone."

Vince Edwards

As Ben Casey, he brought sex appeal (and chest hair) to hospital drama

When Vince Edwards, the swarthy, brooding star of ABC's *Ben Casey* (1961-66), unbuttoned the collar of his medical tunic to expose what he humorously called "wall-to-wall" chest hair, hearts fluttered in Nielsen households. Ben Casey shirts were soon a hot item. The series, realistic for its time, was the high point of Edwards's career. In following years, a gambling habit cost him thousands a day at the track. But by the time he was diagnosed in October '95 with the pancreatic cancer that would kill him in five months, Edwards, 67, had his gambling under control and his life together. "He was determined to be a role model," says Janet, his third wife, whom he married in 1994.

Tupac Shakur

He lived and died by the message of his music

He rapped his way from poverty to riches, but the themes of the chart-breaking songs that made the career of Tupac Amaru Shakur were always violent ones. Those were also the themes of the life of the gangsta rapper and actor, who spookily prophesied his own demise in his music. Hits like "Death Around the Corner" and "If I Die 2Nite," from his platinum 1995 release, *Me Against the World*, as well as his last music video, *I Ain't Mad at Cha*, in which he is shot and goes to heaven, foreshadowed his own end at age 25—gunned down in a drive-by shooting near the Las Vegas strip. He "knew intuitively that he wasn't going to live a long time," says Rev. Herbert Daughtry, a Brooklyn minister since childhood.

Two years ago he was robbed, beaten and shot five times outside a Manhattan recording studio while awaiting the verdict and eventual 11-month sentence he served for sexually abusing a fan. The experience was almost like a trophy for Shakur, who bragged on his record *All Eyez on Me*: "Five shots and they still couldn't kill me." But the four bullets that struck him this time could. When Shakur left a Mike Tyson fight as a passenger in the BMW of Marion "Suge" Knight, the head of Shakur's Death Row Records label, an unknown assailant unleashed a fusillade and sped away. Knight was barely grazed, but Shakur lay in a coma for almost a week before he finally died. Khalid Shah, an L.A. antiviolence activist, hoped that would end the cycle of revenge. "Maybe," he said, "his death will be a way of saying it's time for the madness to stop."

Dorothy Lamour

The glamor girl in the sarong, a longtime sidekick of Hope and Crosby, reaches the end of the road

Dorothy Lamour, born 81 years ago in a New Orleans charity ward, first swung into the limelight in 1936's *The Jungle Princess*, clad in the clingy sarong that became her trademark. A favorite WWII GI pinup, the sultry brunette was so successful a War Bonds saleswoman that a private railroad car was put at her disposal. Seven gigs with Bob Hope and Bing Crosby, from 1940's *Road to Singapore* to '62's *The Road to Hong Kong*, made her, in her words, "the happiest and highest-paid straight woman in the business."

Don Simpson

A Hollywood fantasist
self-destructed

"I grew up with no magic in my life," Don Simpson once mused, looking back on his strict Christian fundamentalist upbringing. "All I wanted to be was a magician." Simpson found his wand when Paramount hired him as a development assistant in 1976. Seven years later, he and Jerry Bruckheimer formed a production company—and released a string of pictures that mirrored the mood of the go-go times. Collectively, *Flashdance, Beverly Hills Cop* and its sequel, plus *Top Gun* grossed $1.4 billion worldwide. Unfortunately, money fueled addiction to the darker magic of megasuccess. When Simpson, 52, died accidentally from a combination of cocaine, sedatives, antidepressants and antipsychotic medications, friends were saddened but not surprised. Observed MCA's Tom Pollack, a longtime pal: "Don pushed the envelope always, and the envelope pushed back."

Erma Bombeck

Her dishpan hands proudly
turned chores into chuckles

In 1964, after the last of her three children started elementary school, Erma Bombeck, then 37, decided she was "too old for a paper route, too young for Social Security and too tired for an affair." So she persuaded the editor of a suburban weekly near her home in Centerville, Ohio, to pay her $3 a column for a running commentary on domestic life.

Syndicated within a year and carried by some 700 newspapers by the time she died at 69 of complications following a long-awaited kidney transplant, Erma Bombeck's *At Wit's End* was an installment epic, chronicling her quotidian struggles with ironing boards piled high, teen offspring who withdrew to their rooms seemingly for years at a stretch and males who incorrigibly left the toilet seat up. "How would men like it if they got up in the middle of the night and groped their way down a dark hallway," she wrote, "only to fall down a dark, bottomless hole like Alice in Wonderland?"

Though made wealthy by her column, TV appearances and a dozen books with such titles as *The Grass is Always Greener Over the Septic Tank* (1976) and *I Lost Everything in the Post-Partum Depression* (1986), Bombeck discarded neither mop nor broom nor husband Bill, 69, a school principal. "If I didn't do my own housework, then I have no business writing about it," she said. "I spend 90 percent of my time living scripts and 10 percent writing them." Commented her friend, columnist Art Buchwald, "That stuff wouldn't work if it was jokes. What it was, was the truth."

Charlie O. Finley

A combative showman
updated major league ball

An obstreperous baseball owner with a genius for promotion, Charles O. Finley, 77, would've been on *Seinfeld* if it had been around in his heyday. He hired and fired, innovated and resisted innovation with a fury that built a three-peat (1972-74) World Championship for the Oakland A's—then lost it all to free agency, which he fought unsuccessfully in the courts. His chief legacy: the American League's designated hitter, which added new sock to the sport.

William Colby

An ex-spymaster departs in a cloak of mystery

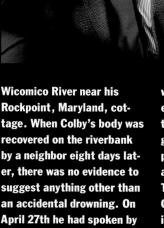

It was a conspiracy theorist's field day. Ex-CIA director Bill Colby, 76—who had broken the spy's code of silence and testified to Congress about the Agency's illegal activities, including domestic snooping—had vanished. On April 28, his overturned canoe was found washed up on a beach of the Wicomico River near his Rockpoint, Maryland, cottage. When Colby's body was recovered on the riverbank by a neighbor eight days later, there was no evidence to suggest anything other than an accidental drowning. On April 27th he had spoken by phone with his wife Sally, 51, a foreign aid official who was at a Houston conference, telling her that although it was windy, he was going canoeing—a favorite pastime. "It may have been an accident," says Joseph Trento, author of *Widows*, a Cold War history. "But this is a guy who had enemies because they thought he shot off his mouth to Congress."

Bill Monroe

He gave America a scintillating new sound—bluegrass

A cantankerous mandolin player with a keening tenor, Bill Monroe created an American folk-art form—a vibrant blend of Appalachian mountain melodies, blues, gospel and jazz that took its name from his band, the Blue Grass Boys. He sold 40 million records, influencing everyone from Elvis Presley (who turned Monroe's "Blue Moon of Kentucky" into his first regional hit) to Bob Dylan. Monroe, who died of a stroke at 84, "put his whole life in the music," said his onetime banjo man, Earl Scruggs. Some say he gave the music a whole new life, too.

Claudette Colbert

She could play a siren or a screwball, or both at once

As a runaway heiress thumbing a lift in Frank Capra's *It Happened One Night*, Claudette Colbert raised her skirt and let her legs stop traffic. Equally arresting were her box-office "legs." The doe-eyed, Parisian-born actress, who died at 92, starred in movies spanning six decades, including spectacles *(Cleopatra*, right), World War II weepies *(So Proudly We Hail)*, and—most famously— comedies *(Bluebeard's Eighth Wife, The Palm Beach Story)*. Her second marriage also had legs, lasting 33 years until her husband, Dr. Joel Pressman, died in 1968.

"She had no airs about her," recalls Ann-Margret, her costar in her final role, the 1986 miniseries *The Two Mrs. Grenvilles.* But Colbert was no pushover on the set. While filming *It Happened One Night*, she sparred often with the director, most notably over her reluctance to raise her skirt (she yielded only when a chorus girl was called in to "double" for her). When Colbert collected the 1934 Best Actress Oscar for the role, she said, with typical grace, "I owe Frank Capra for this."

Mike Boorda

His suicide reflected the riptides
roiling the post-Tailhook Navy

He was the only swabbie ever to rise to the Navy's
highest uniformed post. Chief of Naval Operations
Jeremy "Mike" Boorda, who grew up in small-town
Illinois the grandson of Ukrainian Jewish immigrants, epitomized the triumph of hard work over
hardship. Lying about his age so he could enlist at
16, Boorda eventually skippered ships, did two
tours in Vietnam, served at the Pentagon and led
NATO forces in southern Europe. Among the en-
listed men and women, well aware he came from
their ranks, he was a popular hero. "This guy got
along with his troops as well as Colin Powell,"
says Harlan Ullman, a retired Navy commander
and friend.

Yet Boorda's ebullient persona belied a troubled
soul. There were pressures stemming from Naval
Academy cheating scandals, aircraft crashes and,
particularly, the aftermath of Tailhook. Old guard
officers complained that his administration was
too conciliatory and political in trying to redress
the service's history of sexual harassment. "Like

the father of a family, Boorda took these problems
personally," says former Assistant Secretary of
Defense Lawrence Korb. Boorda had also faced
significant personal trauma. The first of his four
children, David, was born with Goltz syndrome, a
rare congenital disorder that causes malformation
of limbs and organs. In spite of advice that they
institutionalize him, Boorda and his wife Bettie
saw him through 17 operations by the time he was
4 and insisted on raising David at home. "You
have to deal with it every day," Boorda once said.
"Not just every day for a little while, but forever."

But service mates were disbelieving when Boorda, 56, committed suicide in May during a lunch
break, with a bullet from a .38-cal. pistol. The final straw seemed to be hearing that reporters
sought to question him about two bronze V's—indicating combat experience—that he'd worn, perhaps improperly, over the years.

Yet were these difficulties enough to push an
outwardly cheerful military leader, who often
made self-deprecating jokes about his stature
(5'4"), to take his own life? Says Harlan Ullman, a
retired commander and Boorda associate who is
now a senior fellow at the Center for Strategic and
International Studies: "If I had 27 advanced degrees, and if you gave me a zillion dollars, I still
couldn't write a paper as to why this happened."

Spiro Agnew

Nixon's hit man went quietly into the footnotes of history

It was the fulfillment of the American dream . . . almost. Spiro Agnew, son of a Greek immigrant peddler, became Vice President. Plucked from relative obscurity by President Richard Nixon, the Maryland governor was the Administration point man in its war against liberals, anti-Vietnam war activists, the media and all enemies, real and perceived. "It was a very controversial period," says Victor Gold, his press secretary, "and Agnew was at its vortex." But 10 months before he would have succeeded Nixon in the wake of Watergate, Agnew himself had to resign when he pleaded no contest to charges of income-tax evasion related to kickbacks taken as a state official. By the time he died at 77, he had become a historical footnote, having lived 23 years out of the public eye.

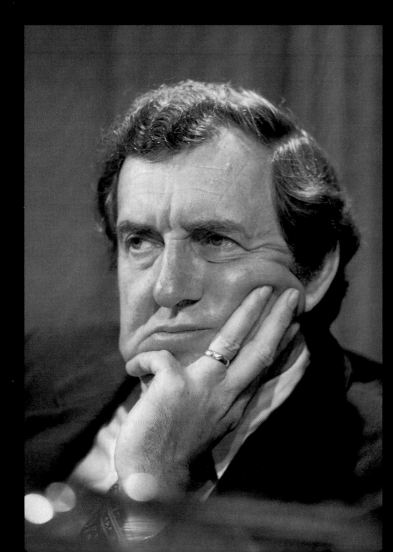

Edmund Muskie

Maine's principled senator may have made a fine President

On a snowy day in 1972, Sen. Edmund Muskie of Maine, front-runner in the New Hampshire Democratic presidential primary, stood outside the offices of *The Union Leader* in Manchester and called its publisher "a gutless coward" for printing scurrilous rumors that Muskie's wife, Jane, drank too much and told dirty jokes. Then the craggy, 6'4" politician appeared to weep in anger. Today, when tear ducts are instruments of spin control, it's stunning to recall that Muskie's spontaneous display shattered his candidacy.

The loss may have been the nation's. A man of powerful intellect, energy and integrity, Muskie was instrumental in crafting the 1963 Clean Air Act and the 1965 Water Quality Act, two linchpins of environmental protection. Muskie's death at 81 cast a long shadow over a political era of easy tears and facile promises.

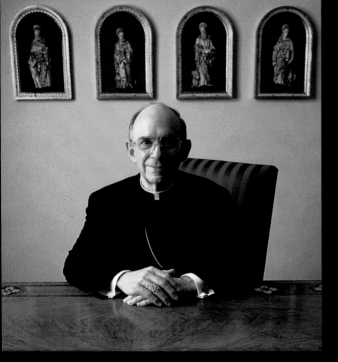

Cardinal Bernardin

An admired Roman Catholic leader demonstrates how to die with grace

He inspired people of many faiths, not only with the dignity with which he lived his life but also how he left it. With death finally near after a painful, 17-month struggle with pancreatic cancer, the Archbishop of Chicago, Cardinal Joseph Bernardin, 68, said he believed that "sometimes we accomplish the greatest good when we are suffering." Over 250,000 attended the three-day visitation at Chicago's Holy Name Cathedral before his November burial to mourn the loss of a spiritual peacemaker who had won praise for his common touch and for his liberal voice on such controversial issues as AIDS. The son of poor Italian immigrants who settled in South Carolina, Bernardin became at 38 the youngest Catholic bishop in the U.S. Accused of sexually abusing former seminarian Stephen Cook in 1993, Bernardin calmly denied the charges until they were recanted four months later. The following year, he said mass for Cook, who had died of AIDS. "He brought light" said one admirer at Bernardin's funeral, "to a world that has settled for semidarkness."

Alger Hiss

Soviet spy or scapegoat of anti-Red hysteria, he divided Cold War America

Even after his death of emphysema at 92, Alger Hiss remains a national litmus test. Conservatives believe him a traitor who spied for the Soviets before World War II. Liberals feel he was a martyr to anti-Red hysteria and to the ambition of an until-then-obscure congressman, Richard Nixon. Whether his 1948 accuser, TIME editor (and turncoat Communist courier) Whittaker Chambers, had it right is still disputed. But Hiss —a patrician lawyer who clerked for Justice Oliver Wendell Holmes, served the New Deal and was an architect of the United Nations—did 44 months in prison for perjury. Disbarred and disgraced, he spent the next 20 years as a stationery salesman. His wife, Priscilla, lost her teaching job, and the marriage ended. Readmitted to the bar, he appealed his conviction unsuccessfully, but recalls his writer son Tony: "My father was the most unbitter man I ever knew."

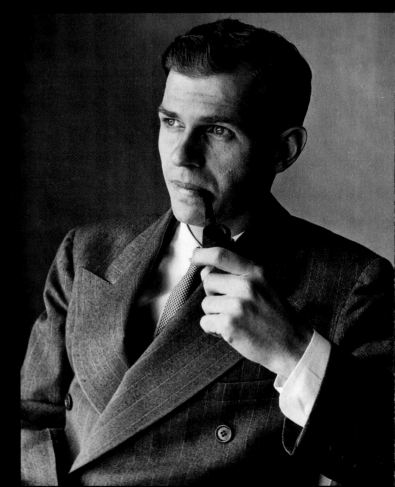

François Mitterrand

The French statesman overcame a Vichy past to strive for European unity and a new Paris

In 14 years as President of France, François Mitterrand, 79, (leaving office in 1995, above) made European unity—cemented by close Franco-German collaboration—his cause. He may have been driven by a desire to atone for a different kind of collaboration: his participation in the Nazi-controlled Vichy government. Late in life, Mitterrand allowed a biographer to reveal this aspect of his past—along with his youthful participation in ultranationalist groups and his fathering a daughter outside his marriage of 52 years. In 1995, he co-authored *Memoirs in Two Voices* with Holocaust survivor and Nobel Peace Laureate Elie Wiesel, to whom he said that the sight of French Jews forced to wear a yellow star spurred him to reject Vichy and join the French Resistance in 1943.

One of eight children of an aviation executive, Mitterrand grew up steeped in Catholicism and the classics. When he won the presidency on his third try in 1981, the socialist Mitterrand lurched the country left. But after a Clintonesque midterm rebuff, he embraced key goals of his former rival, Charles de Gaulle, including an ambitious makeover of Paris. On his watch were built a vast new National Library and a revitalized Louvre, fronted by I.M. Pei's luminous frame-and-glass pyramid.

Mary Leakey

Her tireless digging unearthed our African origins

Her taste ran to single-malt Scotches and Cuban cigars, but Mary Leakey wasn't one to pamper herself. The London-born daughter of a landscape painter, she spent her life toiling in the African sun. The fossils she found proved that humans had emerged in Africa, not Asia, and that hominids had walked erect more than 3 million years ago. A gifted scientist though she never finished high school, Leakey frowned on the self-promotion of her famous fossil-hunting husband, Louis, and they separated in 1968. Her three sons, including paleontologist Richard, live in Kenya, where Mary died at 83.

Tiny Tim

Sincerity was his strangest and most touching quality

His act hadn't changed much since the '60s—strum the ukulele, warble oldies and kick out with his trademark "Tip-toe Thru' the Tulips with Me." It was his biggest hit, in 1968, and singing it was the last thing he would ever do. Moments after leaving the stage at a Minneapolis fund-raiser, Tiny Tim, 64, died of a heart attack. "The last sound he heard was the audience's applause," said Sue Gardner-Khaury, 41, his third wife.

The man born Herbert Khaury in New York City lived for that sound. Enthralled with vaudeville, he perfected his quavering falsetto and bizarre look in Times Square. An early manager, who had worked with midgets, dubbed him Tiny Tim. It became a household name in 1968, when his remake of the 1929 ditty "Tip-toe" reached No. 17. The next year, Tiny's wedding to Vicki Budinger on Johnny Carson's show (above) became one of the most watched events in TV history. (Their daughter, Tulip, 25, is a Pittsburgh homemaker.) Ensuing years would dim Tiny's fame and health, but he never tired of performing. He was buried in Minneapolis, alongside his beloved ukulele.

Joseph Brodsky

The expelled Soviet "parasite" became U.S. Poet Laureate

In 1964, Russian poet Joseph Brodsky was sentenced to five years' hard labor for "parasitism"—the Soviets feared his growing popularity and persecuted him as a Jew. In 1972, they expelled him. By the time he died of a heart attack in his Brooklyn home, Brodsky, 55, had found much honor outside his native land, winning the Nobel Prize for Literature in 1987 and becoming Poet Laureate of his adoptive country in 1991.

Harold Brodkey

He devoted 31 pages to a sexual act
—and 32 years to a novel

Was the fiction writer and essayist Harold Brodkey "an American Proust" or the perpetrator of an "endless kvetch"? Critics labeled him both, and with some justice. He was a formidably gifted stylist who had been a spoiled and troubled child, haunted by the early loss of his mother and the serious illnesses of both adoptive parents. Brodkey wrote a tortured, introspective prose that frankly recorded, among other intimacies, a "binary" sexual phase, to which he attributed the AIDS that took his life at 65. His best-known piece, the 1973 short story "Innocence," devoted 31 pages to a single sexual act. Writing for Brodkey was a similarly drawn-out process: His long-anticipated magnum opus, the novel *The Runaway Soul* took him 32 years to write, sustained by advances from at least five publishers. When it was finally published in 1991, reviewer D.M. Thomas called it "monstrous, ambitious, bold and puzzling" —words that might serve as Brodkey's epitaph.

Jessica Mitford

The late-blooming author dug up the dirt on undertakers

Death became her. In her 1963 best-seller, *The American Way of Death*, muckraking British author Jessica Mitford indicted the funeral business for putting over "a huge, macabre and expensive practical joke on the American public"—needless embalmings, inflated costs and euphemisms that transformed corpses into "loved ones," coffins into "caskets" and undertakers into "funeral directors." The controversial book, which suggested dead bodies should be donated to medical schools instead of buried, eventually prompted a federal investigation of the industry.

Mitford, who died of lung cancer at 78 at her home in Oakland, California, did not become a writer until she was 38. Born to titled parents, she eloped at 19 with a second cousin and was cut out of her father's will. She and her husband came to America, and after he was killed in WWII she tried union organizing and bartending before picking up the pen. Exposing the underside of institutions we take for granted became Mitford's mission. She took on prisons, birth in America (she found cesareans too preva-

lent) and even the British aristocracy— the latter in an autobiography about her large and eccentric family. Asked once what sort of funeral she would want, the irreverent and witty polemicist said she'd like one with "six black horses, with plumes and one of those marvelous embalming jobs that takes twenty years off."

Minnie Pearl

Cornball, though not to the core, she served
up a heap o' hillbilly humor for a mere $1.98

Her signature line was a cackling, "How-deeee!" But Sarah
Ophelia Colley Cannon was vastly different from the gleeful
bumpkin—known to the world as Minnie Pearl—she played
on Nashville's Grand Ole Opry beginning in 1940 and from
1970 to 1991 on TV's *Hee-Haw*. The youngest of five children
born to an affluent lumber dealer in Centerville, Tenn., Sarah

ing the stage with Katharine Hepburn. Articulate and well-
read, she later became a community leader, working tire-
lessly for charity.

Cannon created the Minnie Pearl persona—with trademark $1.98 price tag dangling from her hat—quite deliber-
ately, her imagination fired by a former landlady with a brood
of 16 kids and a knack for storytelling. She and her husband
and manager of 49 years, Henry Cannon, had no children,
and she often spoke of Minnie with pride: "She's apple pie
and clothes dried in the sun and the smell of fresh bread bak-
ing. I don't think people think of her so much as a show-
business act as a friend." When Cannon died in Nashville
of a stroke at 83, country fans felt they had lost a dear old

René Lacoste

A canny, on-court strategist also had a head for sporting goods and duds

His playing career lasted barely nine years way back in the 1920s, but René Lacoste left his mark forever on tennis and preppy attire. After taking up the sport late at 15, he developed a masterful tactical and baseline game that led to two Wimbledon and two U.S. Open titles. "This was one of the finest tennis brains I ever encountered," said Bill Tilden, after Lacoste's French team took home the 1927 Davis Cup. Known as Le Crocodile for his on-court tenacity, Lacoste had a keen business brain too, eventually embroidering that reptilian emblem on a line of sportswear that became an international craze. He also pioneered a ball-lobbing machine and, in 1964, perfected the metal, open-throat tennis racket. When he died, following surgery for a broken leg, Lacoste was at work on patenting further racket refinements. He was 92.

Pierre Franey

A great chef and teacher democratized haute cuisine for a nation of gourmands on the go

His love of food was so obvious that his family was already calling him Pierre le Gourmand at the tender age of 5. Later he was anointed with an even better title: *The Sixty-Minute Gourmet.* Franey and his longtime kitchen partner, *New York Times* food columnist Craig Claiborne, produced a weekly column (and six bestselling *Sixty-Minute Gourmet* volumes) that simplified the fundamentals of fine cooking for eat-and-run Americans. Franey, 75, produced a memoir and seven other cookbooks, mostly with cowriters, and in the '80s brought his expertise and enthusiasm to television. Claiborne once wrote that he thought Franey "a veritable Merlin . . . in knowing precisely how to make a culinary catastrophe into a thing of genius."

That genius was noted by many others, including top military brass during WWII when the young Burgundy-born chef was invited to be General MacArthur's personal cook (he declined). Franey met his wife, Betty, in France in 1947, and they raised three children. She was with him on board the QE2, en route to England, when he suffered a stroke after giving a cooking demonstration.

Dr. Haing S. Ngor
Crime claims a survivor of genocide

Imprisoned by Cambodia's murderous Khmer Rouge regime in its campaign against the educated elite during the 1970s, Dr. Haing S. Ngor survived incessant torture and endured the deaths of most of his family. Arriving in L.A. in 1980 with $4 in his pocket, the gynecologist built a remarkable new life— winning an Oscar for his role in *The Killing Fields* and investing in Cambodian rebuilding efforts. His survivor's spirit was snuffed out when Ngor, 50ish, was accosted in an alley in L.A.'s Chinatown—and shot when he refused to give up a locket bearing a picture of his late wife. She herself had been a Khmer Rouge victim, dying in his arms while in labor because he lacked surgical instruments.

Barbara Jordan
Her booming oratory brought an impassioned conscience to the fore in Texas and the nation

As legislator and legal scholar, Barbara Jordan carried a copy of the Constitution in her purse. She did note, though, that she "felt that George Washington and Alexander Hamilton just left me out by mistake. But," she added, "through the process of amendment, interpretation and court decision I have finally been included in 'We, the people.'" As the first African-American woman ever elected to Congress from the South, Jordan left a legacy of greater inclusion.

Gender and race boundaries never held back the Houston ghetto-born daughter of a Baptist minister, and in 1966, she became Texas's first black state senator and, six years later, speaker pro tem. She went to Capitol Hill in 1972, arguing for the impeachment of Richard Nixon while on the House Judiciary Committee and then memorably keynoting (below) the 1976 Democratic National Convention. Confined to a wheelchair by multiple sclerosis, she left the House to become professor of political ethics at the University of Texas government school named for her mentor, Lyndon B. Johnson. Declared Texas Gov. George W. Bush at her death at 59: "Texas has lost a powerful voice of conscience and integrity."

Frances Lear

A militant muse, the mold for TV's Maude, became a voice for feminism in her own right

She was the model for Maude, the tart-tongued sitcom feminist created by her ex-husband Norman Lear in the '70s (and played by Bea Arthur). When the pair divorced in 1986, Frances collected a $112 million settlement from the TV writer-megaproducer and put a chunk of it into *Lear's*, the first magazine aimed at women over 40. Part service, part soapbox, the monthly lasted through six years of staff storm and turnover. "She was a prickly person," conceded even her friend *Cosmopolitan* editor Helen Gurley Brown.

Lear blamed her mercurial manner on manic depression and lithium, the medicine she took to manage it. In her 1992 memoir, *The Second Seduction*, she revealed a host of other woes, ranging from molestation at 12 by a stepfather (she spent her first year in an orphanage), to alcoholism, three attempted suicides and two divorces pre-Norman. The women's movement finally gave her a purpose, and she cofounded an L.A. executive recruitment firm for women and minorities. When she died of breast cancer at 73, ex-husband Lear noted that "she had flamboyance and flair and a taste for elegance rare in this world. She was an original from the day we met until the day the world said goodbye to her."

Jonathan Larson

The creator of *Rent* never lived to see his great Broadway notices or bask in his Pulitzer

No one who knew him ever doubted he had the goods. Jonathan Larson, author of the Pulitzer Prize-winning musical *Rent*, "was always the most talented guy around," recalled Victoria Leacock, 32, a Manhattan filmmaker who was Larson's lover when they were students at Long Island's Adelphi University and a close friend ever since. "The most talented actor in his class and the most talented writer."

That talent came to fruition when *Rent*, a rock-and-rhythm update of Puccini's *La Bohème*, ran at the Off-Broadway New York Theater Workshop to dream reviews. Centered on a group of modern-day bohemians—some of them HIV-positive —in New York City, *Rent* was, in *Newsday*'s words, "the first original breakthrough rock musical since *Hair*." Encouraged by Stephen Sondheim, a mentor, Larson had stuck with composing after Adelphi. *Rent* was his first big success. And tragically, his last. After six years of work on *Rent*, supported by waiting on tables, Larson returned home after the final dress rehearsal on January 25—then collapsed and died of an aortic aneurysm that two hospitals misdiagnosed and that may have been preventable. The January 26 preview performance became a kind of wake, with the *Rent* cast singing the score for Larson's friends and family.

On the night after Larson was posthumously awarded the Pulitzer and shortly before the Broadway opening, seven of his friends huddled at a Manhattan bistro. "It's hard," said ex-flame Leacock. "I'm going to be celebrating with friends tonight, and he's not there, and it's all wrong." Says Jonathan's father, Al Larson, a retired business executive who lives with Jonathan's mother, Nanette, in New Mexico: "He had terrific friends and he loved the theater. He should be here for this. He worked hard for it."

Johnny "Guitar" Watson

The Gangster of Love made his six-string a lethal weapon

When he performed in Carnegie Hall in 1977, Johnny "Guitar" Watson strutted in a skintight sequined suit and plucked the punchy guitar riffs that caused the French to nickname him the Godfather of Funk. For most of his career, however, Watson, who died of a heart attack at 61 after a performance in Japan, had a very different style, playing steamy rhythm-and-blues. Luscious and sexual hits like "Booty Ooty" and "Hot Little Mama" earned him a different moniker during that time—the "Gangster of Love." Watson, who learned piano as a child from his father, made his first record at 18. He vanished from the music scene in the late '70s and '80s, then re-emerged in 1994 with a hit single, "Bow Wow." Frank Zappa had a description for Watson's unique sound on guitar, which he sometimes used on his records: "An icepick to the forehead."

Morey Amsterdam

He billed himself as the Human Joke Machine, and he was not exaggerating

Morey Amsterdam, who died in Los Angeles at 87, was a gifted gag writer for everyone from Will Rogers and Fanny Brice to Presidents Roosevelt and Reagan. The son of a violinist, he joked his way from vaudeville to Vegas, from radio to TV, where he starred on game shows like *Hollywood Squares* and *Broadway Open House*, a *Tonight* precursor. A father of two who was married to wife Kay for more than 50 years, Amsterdam once even had his own TV variety hour called *Stop Me if You've Heard This One*. But he was best known as Buddy Sorrell on the *Dick Van Dyke Show*, in which he played, aptly, the leader of a team of comedy writers. "When Morey died," said Van Dyke, "a hundred thousand jokes went with him."

135

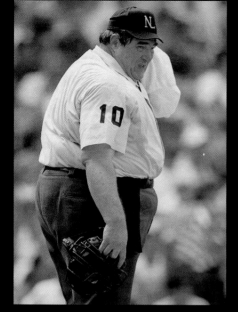

John McSherry

In an Opening Day shocker, the umpire died at the job he loved

"Eddie, you can call the first two innings," joked veteran ump John McSherry, 51, to Cincinnati Reds' catcher Eddie Taubensee, as both crouched for the first pitch of the Reds' 1996 season. But the Opening Day game never got that far. After the seventh pitch, McSherry called time out, began to walk toward the backstop—then staggered and collapsed of a heart attack. Umpires, ballplayers and 53,000 fans looked on in disbelief as efforts to restart his heart— weakened by job stress and by carrying his nearly 400-lb. frame—failed.

Richie Phillips of the Major League Umpires' Association noted McSherry's fatalism: "He'd say, 'If I'm going to go, I'd rather go on a baseball diamond.' " In his 26 years in the major leagues, McSherry had won the players' respect—in part because he would admit when he missed a call. "He was a sweet man," said Mark Grace of the Chicago Cubs. "I had to fight back the tears." Marion Doyle, 42, who had shared a home with McSherry since 1989, made the final call: "He was the most gentle and giving man you would ever meet."

Albert R. Broccoli

The producer gave Agent 007 his license to thrill

James Bond, the dashing British spy who likes his martinis shaken and his women stirring, owes his suave screen existence to a man whose childhood chubbiness earned him the lifelong nickname "Cubby." A descendant of the Italian agronomist who reportedly developed the vegetable bearing the lineal name, Albert Romolo Broccoli began his career in the family vegetable business, then tried another family enterprise, coffin making, which he found depressing. Visiting a cousin who was a Hollywood agent, the engaging young man happened to meet Cary Grant, and they became friends. Broccoli found a job in the mailroom of 20th Century Fox, worked on a few films, eventually became an agent and then produced films in England. With partner Harry Saltzman he optioned the rights to the spy novels of Ian Fleming, but could not get financing because the James Bond character was thought too British and sexually rapacious. Finally, United Artists put up $1 million, which the team turned into 1962's *Dr. No*, the first of 17 Bond thrillers Broccoli would produce before he died at 87. But it was Broccoli's wife of 37 years, Dana, who got credit for the discovery of Sean Connery, who became the first 007. Seeing the unknown actor in a clip, she told her husband, "Take that one! He's gorgeous!"

Minnesota Fats

Fats's city was wherever there was a dollar to be hustled

He claimed he had been around the world six times, could whistle in five languages and had beaten Adolf Hitler at pool. But in a lifetime of hustling, his greatest trick had been a personal one: the transformation of Rudolf Wanderone Jr., a New York City boy, into pool shark and legend spinner Minnesota Fats. In and out of the pool halls where he plied his trade, Minnesota Fats, who died of congestive heart failure at home in Nashville, was the master of applied psychology. "He'd hustle you out of a cookie, if he thought you wanted it," said Teresa Bell Wanderone, 40, his second wife and widow.

"The pool table was my crib," Fats once said. Born in either 1900 or 1913 (a matter of dispute) to poor Swiss immigrant parents in Manhattan, he learned the game by age 5 and dropped out of school at 13 to pursue higher education in Times Square pool parlors. Soon he was traveling in search of com-petition and "tomatoes" (as he called women) and bringing home the bacon with astounding regularity. "When he got in a game," says first wife Evelyn, 78, who was divorced from Fats in 1985, "I just sat with my hands folded and knew it was money in the bank." Even his name was a hustling prize. Known as New York Fats early in his career, he as-serted that the Jackie Gleason title character in the 1961 movie *The Hustler* was based on him. Sensing promotional opportunity, he usurped the name and racked himself up as Minnesota Fats.

Melvin Belli

To the showboating King of Torts, all the legal world was his stage

A flamboyant, silver-maned attorney whose reso-nant voice was compared to a symphony orchestra, Melvin Belli represented luminaries like Mae West, Lenny Bruce and Jim Bakker. For his suc-cess in personal-injury cases, he was dubbed the King of Torts and claimed to have won settlements totaling $600 million. On behalf of a young moth-er whose leg was severed by a San Francisco trol-ley, he sat in court with an ominous, elongated package. Only in summation did he reveal its con-tents—an artificial limb—which he proceeded to drop on the lap of a juror. But after a life of carousing with clients like Errol Flynn and six mar-riages, he died following a stroke at 88, amid mal-practice charges and having filed for bankruptcy.

Juliet Prowse

She made high-kicking headlines with
Khrushchev, Presley and Sinatra

Juliet Prowse became famous overnight in 1959
when Soviet leader Nikita Khrushchev visited the
Hollywood set of *Can-Can* and, in a bit of diplo-
matic grandstanding, called her performance
"immoral." "Let's face it," said the dancer-
actress, "the cancan is a pretty raucous number.
It's not exactly *Swan Lake*." Before her death at
59 of pancreatic cancer, Prowse starred in both
worlds, having been a prima ballerina with the Fes-
tival Ballet of Johannesberg at 14 after leaving her
native Bombay. Discovered in Europe by choreographer Hermes Pan, she built a solid career in
road companies of musicals like *Mame* and as a
Las Vegas headliner. Audiences loved her sassy,
high-kicking style, and she was also a favorite of
the tabloids after a six-week engagement to Frank
Sinatra in 1962 and a fling with Elvis Presley.

Don McNeill

His folksy style defined talk radio when
America marched to a less martial drummer

Before Leno and Letterman, before Carson, before even
Arthur Godfrey, Don McNeill was the prototype of broadcast
hosts, a Homer of homespun talk radio. He was a gregarious
fellow who would chat up his hodgepodge of guests, trade
puns and wisecracks with his bandleader and, when things
got slow, cheerfully stomp through the studio audience.
Indeed, at 15-minute intervals, everyone would get up and
march around his proverbial breakfast table.

The Breakfast Club premiered on network radio in 1933,
and his rotating cast included Fran Allison (of *Kukla, Fran
and Ollie*) and Jim and Marian Jordan (better known as Fibber
McGee and Molly). But McNeill really brought the show to life
when he tossed the script and interviewed audience members
who would pilgrimage to his Chicago set by the busload.
They read their poetry and recipes, and shared inspirational
moments. Born in Galena, Illinois, McNeill never lost his midwestern twang or folksy charm, and somehow managed to
rule radio through the early years of TV and to stay on the air
until 1968. By then, America marched to a more martial
drummer, and contention outrated congeniality. But when
McNeill died of apparent heart failure at 88, his gentle spirit
lived on in Garrison Keillor and enjoyed a veritable renais-
sance in the unassuming bonhomie of Rosie O'Donnell.

Pete Rozelle

A marketing genius changed the national pastime to football

Pete Rozelle, the very model of a modern major-league commissioner, made pro football America's No. 1 spectator sport. A masterful marketeer and dealmaker, he became a principled monarch who could handle the game's colossal egos and take a stand when needed—in 1969, for example, forcing Joe Namath to sell his interest in a nightclub that was a hangout for gamblers. Originally a publicist and only 33 when he took over the NFL as a compromise choice (on the 23rd ballot) in 1960, Rozelle negotiated the merger with the AFL as well as the increasingly lucrative TV contracts that led to the Super Bowl and *Monday Night Football*. By his retirement in 1989, he had more than doubled the team franchises to 28. When he died of brain cancer at 70, Rozelle was still the fan who once said, "I really felt a high at every Super Bowl."

Helen Kushnick

For the ex-manager of Leno and other top comics, a tragic, embattled life ends at 51

Showbiz manager Helen Kushnick was a truck-driver's daughter, with a rage to rise above her East Harlem roots, a keen eye for comic talent and the hardball style to build careers. Her clients included Jimmie Walker, Elayne Boosler and, briefly, David Letterman. But she made her own name with Jay Leno, whom she handled for 17 years from his scrambling days on the club circuit. When he succeeded Johnny Carson, Kushnick became executive producer of the *Tonight* show. But four shaky months later, she was fired, amid reports of tantrums on the set and backfiring tactics to tie up guests exclusively. Kathy Bates played Kushnick in an HBO movie based on *The Late Shift*, a book that led to a Kushnick libel suit and an out-of-court settlement. But the Leno breakup —he did not attend her funeral and had no comment when she died—was only one of many personal losses in the war that was her life. In 1983, her son Samuel died at age 3 after contracting AIDS from a tainted blood transfusion, and six years later, her husband and onetime partner, entertainment lawyer Jerrold Kushnick, died of cancer. Kushnick herself bravely battled breast cancer for nine years until her death at 51.

Gerry Mulligan

He helped light the flame of cool jazz, and made the burliest sax a butterfly

You start with 30 pounds of brass around your neck and a reed jutting at you that looks like it came from a lumberyard. The baritone saxophone is a bruiser, but Gerry Mulligan made it dart and dance like a ballerina. A charter member of the Miles Davis band that challenged the hegemony of bebop in the pivotal 1949-50 *Birth of the Cool* sessions, Mulligan was known for the fluidity and melodic ingenuity of his playing as well as for arrangements that were as sensuous as they were deft. In the '50s, he also pioneered the pianoless quartet, with trumpeter Chet Baker, producing cascades of counterpoint.

Mulligan was battling liver cancer when he died at 68 of complications after surgery for a knee infection. He was a vibrant performer almost to the end—connecting, all-told, with a veritable Who's Who of jazz, including Thelonious Monk, Stan Getz, Paul Desmond, Harry "Sweets" Edison, Mel Tormé, Wynton Marsalis and many others. Pianist John Lewis said Mulligan's influence had "become so general, they won't know to give him credit in the next generation."

Ella Fitzgerald

Sublime of voice and shy of manner, she lifted melodies, and listeners, into flight

Boop-dee-oopie, de-oop-a-dum-dum. The words may have often been nonsensical, but Ella's sound and spirit were always warm and irresistible, whether she was scatting in wordless fancy or tenderly sketching a ballad. Long before Fitzgerald died of complications from diabetes at 79, "She established a style that spread like a forest blaze," says author Norma Miller, 76, who performed with Fitzgerald at Harlem's Savoy Ballroom when both were teenagers. If, as Miller says, "Frank Sinatra was the epitome of the male American singer," then Ella, she adds, "was the female side." Sinatra himself recalls that "Ella was a sweet, shy girl when we met, and she never lost that innocence." Backstage the shy girl loved playing hearts; at home she was addicted to TV soaps and enjoyed being surrounded by her family. Married twice—first, briefly, in the early '40s, and then, from 1947 to 1953, to bassist Ray Brown—Fitzgerald adopted her half sister's son in the late '40s and named him Ray Jr. Born in 1917 in Newport News, Virginia, the singer won an amateur contest in 1934 and was hired by bandleader Chick Webb. She possessed a supple three-octave range, sparkling diction and an effortless sense of swing. While dedicated to melody, she wasn't afraid to break away and improvise, a quality other musicians loved her for. "She was the last of the first team," said composer-producer Quincy Jones. "I'm talking about Ellington, Basie, the ones who invented this music." Ira Gershwin summed it up best: "I never knew how good our songs were until I heard Ella Fitzgerald sing them."

PICTURE CREDITS

COVER JFK Jr. & Carolyn Bessette: Denis Reggie/© 1996 • Rosie O'Donnell: Janette Beckman/Retna Ltd. • Denzel Washington: Ralph Dominguez/Globe Photos • Goldie Hawn: Dave Benett/Globe Photos • Tom Cruise: Rex USA • Kerri Strug: Rick Dimond/Planet Hollywood • Michael J. Fox: George Lange/ABC • **Back Cover** Christopher Reeve: Alex Berliner/Berliner Studio • Amy Van Dyken: Heinz Kluetmeier • Michael Jackson: Scott Downie/Celebrity Photo • **Title Page** Margaux Hemingway: Martin/Sipa • **Table of Contents** Kerri Strug: Ann States/Saba • Brad Pitt & Gwyneth Paltrow: John Paschal/Celebrity Photo

FACE TIME 4-5 David Allen/LGI • 6-7 Matt Mendelson/LGI • 8-9 Laura D. Luongo/Outline • 10-11 Walter Iooss Jr.• 12-13 AP/Wide World/NBC • 14-15 Tom Copeland/Greensboro News Record/Sipa • 16-17 Christopher Little/Outline • 18-19 Alexander Zemlianichenko/AP/Wide World • 20-21 Globe Photos • 22-23 Najlah Feanny/Saba • 24-25 Robin Bowman

HEADLINERS 26-27 Greg Gibson/AP/Wide World (2) • 28 (from top) B. Kraft/Sygma; Ed Geller/Globe; Peter Morgan/Reuters • 29 Harry Benson (top); Christopher Little/Outline • 30 CJ Walker (top); Lynn Johnson • 31 Walter Iooss Jr.• 32 Heinz Kluetmeier • 33 (clockwise, from top left) Bill Frakes; Manny Millan; Bill Collier/AFP • 34 Steve Adams/Gamma Liaison (left); AP • 35 Rick Wilking/Reuters (left); Brad Rickerby/Sipa • 36 Ann States/Saba • 37 Jim McHugh/Outline • 38 AP/Wide World/FBI • 39 Bebeto Matthews/AP/Wide World (top); Colin Braley • 40 Fitzroy Barrett/Globe Photos • 41 Jonathan Exley/Gamma Liaison • 42 Sam Sargent/Gamma Liaison • 43 Lacy Atkins/AP/Wide World (left); John Storey • 44 Clark Jones/AP/Wide World (top); Steve Kagan • 45 Stephen Alvarez/National Geographic Image Collection • 46-47 Thomas England • 48 J. Allen Hansley • 49 John Zich (top); Bill Lambert • 50 AP/Wide World/WABC-TV (left); Nina Berman/Sipa • 51 David Hartley/Rex USA • 52 J. Scott Applewhite/AP/Wide World (top); Erik C. Pendzich/Rex USA • 53 NASA • 54 Heinz Kluetmeier • 55 Caryn Levy (top); John Mantel/Sipa

SENSATIONS 56-57 Alex Berliner/Berliner Studio • 58 Bob Strong/Sipa (top); Korba/South Beach Photo • 59 Frank Veronsky (top); Mario Ruiz (5), • 60 Lisa Rose/Globe Photos • 61 Armando Gallo/Retna Ltd. • 62 Neal Peters Collection (top); Michael Yarish/MTV • 63 Jack Smith/AP/Wide World •64 Kimberly Butler • 65 Eric Liebowitz/ Warner Bros.• 66 Timothy White/ABC (top); Lisa O'Connor/Celebrity Photo • 67 Marc Asnin/Saba (top); Frank Veronsky • 68 Steven Labadessa (top); Eric L. Williams/Atlanta Journal-Constitution/AP/Wide World • 69 Peter Serling • 70 Acey Harper (top); Lisa Means • 71 Kevin Cummins/London Features • 72 Fred Prouser/Sipa • 73 Gerry Gropp (top); Acey Harper • 74 Andy Schwartz/Paramount Pictures • 75 Robin Bowman (top); Will Hart • 76 The John F. Kennedy Library (top); John Loengard •77 Justin Sutcliffe/Sipa (top); Richard Young/Rex USA, © Caroline Kennedy, John F. Kennedy Jr. and the Estate of Jacqueline Kennedy Onassis; Mark Shaw/Photo Researchers

STYLE 78 (clockwise, top left) Steve Granitz/Retna Ltd.(2); John Paschal/Celebrity Photo • 79 Barron Claiborne/Outline • 80 Lisa Rose/Globe Photos (left); F. Trapper/Sygma; Steve Trupp/Celebrity Photo; Ron Davis/Shooting Star; Albert Ortega/Celebrity Photo; Rex USA; Ctsy of Hush Puppies • 81 (clockwise, left) Barry King/Gamma Liaison; Jim Smeal/Galella Ltd.; Ron Davis/Shooting Star; Bill Davilla/Retna Ltd.; Fotex/Photoreporters • 82 (clockwise, left) Robin Platzer/Twin Images; Ron Davis/Shooting Star; Steve Granitz/Retna Ltd.; Bill Smith • 83 (clockwise, left) Freeman/Michelson; Ed Geller/Globe Photos; Lisa O'Connor/Celebrity Photo; Jim Smeal/Gallela Ltd. • 84 Antoine Verglas • 85 Daniela Federici

FAMILY MATTERS 86 Thomas England (top); H.H.A./Sipa • 87 Larry Schwartzwald/Sygma • 88 Sipa • 89 Scott Downie/Celebrity Photo • 90 (clockwise, left) Alex Berliner/Berliner Studio; Niviere-Benaroch/Sipa; Charles W. Plant/Sipa • 91 (clockwise, top left) David Benett/Globe Photos; NY Post/Globe Photos; Rossa Cole/Sygma; Bob Olen/NY Post/Sipa • 92 (clockwise, top left) Sean Hahn; S. Senne/Sipa; M. Ferguson/Galella Ltd.; C. Brancu/Retna • 93 (clockwise, top left) Janet Gough/Celebrity Photo; Gregg De Guire/London Features Intl.; Robin Platzer/Twin Images; Lazslo Veres; Frank Trapper/Sygma; Vincent Zuffante/Star File Photo; Lawrence Schwartzwald/Sygma • 94 Jim Smeal/Galella Ltd.• 95 Frederic Stevens/Sipa • 96 Gregg De Guire/London Features Intl. • 97 (clockwise, top left) Guttierez/Sipa; Phil Ramey; Alan Levenson; Albert Ferreira/Globe Photos • 98 (clockwise, top left) Steve Granitz/Retna Ltd.; Henry McGee/Globe Photos; Steve Smith/Outline • 99 (clockwise, top) Barry Talesnick/Retna Ltd., Ares/Camera Press/Retna Ltd., Andrea Renault/Globe Photos • 100 (clockwise; bottom left) Yann Gamblin/Outline; Kevin Winter/Celebrity Photo; Miranda Shen/Celebrity Photo; David Fisher/London Features Intl.; Ron Wolfson/London Features Intl.; Laura Luongo/Outline • 101 (clockwise, top) Jim Smeal/Galella Ltd.; Scott Downie/Celebrity Photo; Jeff Kravitz/Film Magic; F. Prouser/Sipa • 102 Mark Saunders/Big Pictures/South Beach Photo • 103 Jim Bennett/Rex USA • 104 (clockwise, top left) Antony Jones/UK Press; Rex USA; Knotek/Globe Photos; Ken Goff • 105 Big Pictures/South Beach Photos

TRIBUTE 106 Everett Collection • 107 David Guilburt/Outline • 108 Richard A. Bloom/Saba • 109 Kevin Abosch/Shooting Star • 110 Kobal Collection • 111 Kobal Collection • 112 Sunset Blvd/Sygma • 113 Kobal Collection • 114 Everett Collection (top); Scott Downie/Celebrity Photo • 115 Mojgan Azimi/Outline • 116 UPI/Corbis-Bettmann (top); Shooting Star • 117 Lester Glassner Collection/Neal Peters (top); Everett Collection • 118 Jeffrey Newbury/Outline 119 Kobal Collection • 120 Henry Groskinsky (top); Fred Kaplan/Black Star • 121 Lee Balterman • 122 Robert Trippett/Sipa (top); Alan Messer/Rex USA • 123 Cecil B. De Mille/Sipa • 124 Mark D. Faram/Defense News • 125 George Tames/Globe Photos (top); Jim Pickerell/Globe Photos • 126 James Schnepf/Gamma Liaison (top); Leo Rosenthal© Time Inc. • 127 Diego Goldberg/Sygma (top); David Blumenkrantz/Gamma Liaison • 128 NBC/Globe Photos (top); Thomas Victor/TIME • 129 James Hamilton/Sygma (top); Mayotte Magnus/Camera Press/Retna • 130 E.J. Camp/Outline • 131 Shonna Valeska (top); UPI/Corbis Bettmann • 132 Lester Glassner Collection/Neal Peters (top), UPI/Corbis-Bettmann • 133 Wyatt Counts/Outline • 134 Gwendolyn Cates/Sygma • 135 David Corio/Retna Ltd. (top); Photofest • 136 Rim Boyle/AP/Wide World (top); David James/Sygma • 137 Corbis-Bettmann (top); Bill Nation/Sygma • 138 Harry Siskind/Outline (top); Arthur Siegel/LIFE • 139 Gregg De Guire/London Features Intl. (top); Tony Triolo/SI • 140 Carol Friedman/Outline • 141 Frank Driggs Collection

INDEX